Macao

Macao

Philippe Pons

Translated by
SARAH ADAMS

REAKTION BOOKS

Published by Reaktion Books Ltd
79 Farringdon Road, London EC1M 3JU

www.reaktionbooks.co.uk

First published in English 2002

First published in French as *Macao, un éclat d'éternité*
© Editions Gallimard, 1999

English language translation © Reaktion Books 2002

This work has been published with the support of the Centre National
du Livre, French Ministry of Culture

Printed and bound by Biddles Limited, Guildford & King's Lynn

British Library Cataloguing in Publication Data

Pons, Philippe
    Macao. – (Topographics)
    1. Macau (China : Special Administration Region) – History
    2. Macau (China : Special Administration Region) – Social life
    and customs
    I. Title
    951.2′6

ISBN 1 86189 136 9

Be sure to tell them that different cities with the same name sometimes succeed each other on the same site; they're born and they die without ever knowing each other, without any contact between them.

Italo Calvino
Invisible Cities

General view of town and port, 1869.

Macao from Green Island by Thomas Boswall Watson, 1852.

A Book With Ripped Out Pages

Cities are fragile constructions, fluid realities; like a precipitate, they're the result of a constellation of elements converging at a given moment in time. When that precipitate dissolves, the city keeps up appearances like a hive without a queen. It still buzzes, but the heart's gone out of it. Today's Macao is one such vanished city, existing only in the archipelago between memory and imagination. The Macao I want to tell you about is a reinvented city, arising from notes made during my visits over a period of 25 years. A beloved, fascinating city so oppressed by the weight of time it forced one's mind to flit continually between present and past. And yet those muffled echoes resonating in the present were either from an imagined past or else one that you read about in books. In Macao you seemed to encroach on so many people's territory, felt the beating hearts of so many vanished lives, and stumbled across so many ghosts whispering their stories that past and present could only blur.

There are cities whose very name is a springboard for the imagination. Cities or places – like Capri, for example – whose incantatory names suggest myths, legends and stories. Macao was one of those imaginary cities that got under your skin before you'd ever set foot there.

For it was here, at the mouth of the Pearl river that East and West met more than four centuries ago on a tongue of land riven by two deep bays – an isthmus so slender at its base it was likened to a lotus stem with the city for its radiant flower. All the races of the world (or most of them) rubbed shoulders here, mingling, falling in love, tolerating one another's beliefs. This tiny Portuguese enclave (some fifteen square kilometres) in

Chinese territory was the West's richest depot on the other side of the world. More merchandise is said to have passed through Macao than crossed the Rialto Bridge in Venice. It was also the outpost on Asian soil for the Church's mission. A city on the edge of two worlds, a city of exchanges, of bodies and cultures mixing, a community of saints, grasping merchants and adventurers, of exiles and ebony-skinned slaves brought over from Africa, of women from Malacca with golden complexions and long *mantillas* worn Portuguese-style over their hair, Macao was also a hotbed of vice: with its gambling dives and opium houses, coolie markets and villas for the indulgence of secret pleasures, it was a haven for smugglers. Impious and devout, idle and hardworking, frivolous and lethargic, generous and cruel: Macao was all these things, simultaneously or by turns. Then, in the aftermath of the Second World War, as if in need of a rest, it began to doze on the banks of Time.

As well as being the West's first anchorage in China, Macao was also its last in Asia: on 20 December 1999, eleven days before the century's close and two years after the handover of Hong Kong to China, the Portuguese lowered their flag, complying with an agreement entered into in 1987 and modelled on the one established between London and Beijing for the former British colony. Why this date? Probably because the Chinese wanted to settle the matter before the threshold of the millennium, and the Portuguese wanted to be back home in time for Christmas. The city they handed back to China differs little from those cities throughout Asia whose souls have been violated under concrete streams of 'development'.

Wealth and prestige had already deserted this city of illusions and shifting landmarks; but, as recently as ten years ago, history stood still in this time-warp where the upturned eaves of Chinese rooftops with their curved tips stood cheek by jowl with Corinthian columns and the wrought-iron railings of pot-bellied balconies; where effigies of the Virgin Mary were paired with small vermilion altars dedicated to local divinities and bathed in fragrant incense. There was such a fine assimilation of marvels from the furthest ends of the world in this sleepy city that it possessed the holy serenity of a moment that lasts forever. The city's beauty derived from the oppression of time and the enforced slowness of hours passing. Mutilated since the mid-1970s by straight causeways obliterating the natural contours of its coastline, the enclave still retained the charm of those cities that knew how to tame history or at least shy away from its unfolding. As Dominique Fernandez writes of Naples, adapting to the necessities of modern life has for a long time seemed the least of Macao's worries. Another page of history was always on the verge of being turned. And then it *was* turned, suddenly, without due care or consideration.

In the late 1980s Macao was caught up in the turmoil of economic expansion in South China and came under violent attack. It capitulated without putting up a fight. Development prevailed over indifference to a changing world. Even before it was handed back to the motherland, this legendary city was killed off by the battering it had received from Chinese, Taiwanese and Hong Kong capitalists who all 'helped themselves to the city'. China recalls the sacking of the Summer Palace in Beijing by Anglo-French troops in 1860 with a sense of outrage, and with good reason. But it has embarked on the equally shameless destruction of its own past in Macao, where it is undeniably on home ground. The tone was set by erecting a gigantic pale pink-and-white-striped tower facing out to sea, to protect China's shores. Time was when the only monument out of keeping with the noble design of the Praia Grande was the kitsch wedding cake of the Hotel Casino Lisboa. Today, that same building is lost in a cityscape of skyscrapers, high-rise blocks, buildings and bill-boards. Hong Kong? But it's a poor man's Hong Kong, a pauper's. Flanked by an airport built on the sea and bristling with the legacy of speculation in the form of residential complexes that now lie half-empty, the enclave's two charming islands of Taïpa and Coloane are joined by causeways. Speculation has trans-formed this unique city into suburbia-on-sea, and Macao will soon disappear, faster than Venice can sink into its lagoon.

The Portuguese disregarded Macao for so long that Montalto de Jesus, one of the enclave's first historians, suggested in the preface to the second edition of his book published in 1926 that Macao be administered by the League of Nations (this resulted in the book being banned by Lisbon: there were few copies in circulation before Oxford University Press reprinted it in 1984). It was only as their departure beckoned that the Portuguese feverishly began to smarten up what was left and to undertake major restoration work. Certain buildings have been tastefully redecorated, among them the Santa Casa de Misericórdia, the buildings of the Largo Senado, the Clube Militar and the 19th-century patrician houses along the Avenida Conselheiro Ferreira de Almeida. But heritage has been reduced to a backdrop, to a *staging* of the past, and Macao has become the Mediterranean's Disneyland on Chinese soil.

The cultural precipitate that made this city such a unique hybrid resulted from its isolation. This was eroded when the enclave was engulfed by the economic development of South China, and Macao began to lose its inestimable charm as it was picked up again by history. In the streets of a city where your imagination was once free to roam, you now come hard up against reality. Two cities overlie each other: one has almost vanished and requires endless reinvention; the other is so present you have to strain to forget it. Macao is now like an old book whose finest pages have been ripped out.

Of course, the new arrival will find it charming enough. But visitors aren't bewitched from the moment they first set foot in Macao. No longer the magical city it once was, Macao is now a theme park.

Daydreaming on a Terrace

Night dissolves with the first glimmer of dawn, and the city seems to melt into the silt-coloured water of the Pearl river delta. The time-honoured customs of two civilizations are re-enacted in streets still drowsy in the small hours. If the churches are empty as yet, the gambling dives remain crowded. The markets in the Chinese districts stir into life; fresh sticks of incense burn in the temples and in front of small street altars dedicated to local divinities. Dawn in Macao used to conjure up whole centuries. And a listless memory can be tugged away again by the breeze tousling the palm trees on the terrace below.

From a bedroom verandah at the Hotel Bela Vista, I notice the street lamps still lit along the Avenida da República where it hugs the smooth curve of the Praia Grande, snaking down to the foot of Barra Hill in a walkway lined with venerable Indian fig trees. The Portuguese colours fly above the Governor's residence, Santa Sancha Palace, and its old pink walls and white friezes stand out against the dark green of the hillside vegetation.

It was this verdant hill, (now with the white façade of São Lourenço Church in the background, and further off that of São Paulo), that the first navigators saw when they emerged from the labyrinth of islands in the delta: they knew their suffering was over. Their voyage from the banks of the Tagus to those of the Pearl river by way of the Cape of Good Hope (known as the Cape of Storms in those days) was almost at end. What hope and ambition did these Renaissance men – still in the grip of medieval fears – have to possess in order to set sail for distant and unknown lands 'against the winds, against the monsoon and against reason'? They braved the elements, disease and pirates. How many individual exploits made up this collective adventure? They and their descendants built churches and forts, depots and houses, a seminary, a hospital and a theatre on the promontory. Previously, there was just a fishing village known for its temple dedicated to the Sea Divinity, Mazu (A-Ma, in the local dialect) on this tongue of land. The temple was situated on the tip of one of the two deep bays of the isthmus, jutting into the sea as if it were the mainland's final thrust before crumbling into a dusty sprinkling of islands.

In the old days, the approach to Macao was, *a fortiori*, a delight as you boarded one of the old white steamers that took three hours to cover the 65 kilometres separating the enclave from Hong Kong, chugging around Barra Head and in front of A-Ma's Temple before docking alongside the Inner Harbour. An exhilarating departure from the hustle and bustle of the British port gave way to the serene slowness of the crossing. Sailing past countless steep-sloped islands and islets, most of them uninhabited, as well as slow flotillas of boats and junks, helped the traveller leave behind the fast life and Hong Kong's fairytale landscape, and prepare to enjoy the pleasures of the sleepy Portuguese enclave with its appealingly soporific languor.

The old *Fatshan*, which deserved to founder in a typhoon, had been in service for more than 30 years. With its stewards in white uniforms, tinny high-pitched Chinese music, and passengers, some of whom began playing cards as soon as the boat was out of Hong Kong territorial waters, it gave the impression of travelling slowly backwards in time to the monotonous hum of its engines and the regular slap of wave against prow. When the sea unexpectedly took on the silty colour of the Pearl river delta with its heavy crepuscular water, it meant you were getting near. You arrived at dawn if you caught the night boat, just as Portugal's colours of red and green were climbing the sky to the top of the old citadel. A small Mediterranean city appeared before you, its houses in faded pastel shades contrasting with the verdant background of the hills and the

14

azure sky. A bell-tower rose up on one of the hills, on the other soared the dark ramparts of the old fort. Macao came towards you like an old sepia photograph, from a sea of junks with massive stern-castles and sails quivering like autumn leaves, all of them flying the Red Flag emblazoned with China's five stars. After Barra Head, there was a fleet of furtive and clumsily steered sampans to be negotiated. Disembarkation was on the quayside of the Inner Harbour, in the thick of junks berthed end to end as far as the eye could see. They formed an undulating city, bristling with tangled masts. Teeming crowds of men, women and children were forever moving from one bridge to another in that floating metropolis. Lighters would tie up or cast off, endlessly slipping back and forth between the quayside and weather-beaten freighters anchored at the outer reaches of Portuguese territorial waters. A few cable lengths away, across the narrow stretch of sea, lay the People's Republic of China.

Macao in those days seemed to harbour the hopes of several centuries. The city was barely different from that described by Joseph Kessel in the mid-1950s: 'a discreet city in white, [it was] languid and drowsy even in its Chinese district, possessing a bewitching charm. The essence of Portugal seemed to have been magically transported from the Atlantic coast to the furthest tip of Canton's bay . . .'. It was a city that 'assumed the gentle tranquillity of *paseos* in provincial Iberian towns, both in the architecture of its houses, arcades and churches and in the casual gait of its people with their sing-song speech'. The writer deplored, however, the presence of two skyscrapers for being 'extravagant, massive, out of keeping, hideous, and destroying all perspective and harmony'. What adjectives would he need to describe the destruction of Macao today?

In the early 1970s Macao was still 'blessed', a city where 'nothing serious could ever happen', according to W. H. Auden, who turned up in there in 1938, shortly after Shanghai had fallen into Japanese hands. Like a starfish washed up by history on the shores of the Pearl river delta, Macao remained supremely indifferent to such events. The pace of this sleepy

15

city where 'nothing ever happened' seemed set by the serene slowness of rickshaws carrying new arrivals through streets which, in Carlo Levi's pleasing phrase, made up the 'infinite whorl of a seashell bringing back to the ear lost sounds from the sea of time'. Cars were rare then, and rickshaws were practically the only means of transport. After a bumpy start, the barefoot driver would establish a regular peddling rhythm, his neck strained and the small of his back swaying animatedly.

Macao had certainly sprung to life at the time of the Cultural Revolution in 1966–7, when its walls were covered with newspapers: Maoist propaganda featuring unexpectedly next to notices of Mass times. There were demonstrations. Police gunfire resulted in eight deaths. Beijing complained and the Governor was forced to issue a public apology, promising that the police would never again use arms against the people. The fever abated. The event had been 'digested'. Portugal had lost its vestigial authority and prestige for good, and China had proved, if any proof was needed, that it was on home ground. The *coup d'état* of 25 April 1974, which toppled the Caetano regime in Lisbon, shook Macao out of its torpor once more. On receiving the junta's telegram declaring itself in power, the soldiers in the garrison found themselves with weapons in their hands. They soon put them down again. Whom were they supposed to be defending from what? There were no questions asked. The sun was setting on Portugal's vast colonial empire in Africa, but barely an eyebrow was raised among the Chinese in Macao as they watched with sardonic irony the political effervescence the upheavals provoked within the microcosm of the enclave's Portuguese community. Macao had only one abiding fear: *change*. When the young officers sent by Lisbon to de-colonize Macao disembarked in December 1974, their heads brimming with ideas about the 'Carnation Revolution', they were disappointed: no one was waiting to be liberated, and China was not inclined at the time to take over from Portugal. In fact, handing over Macao would risk causing panic among Hong Kong banks and businesses vital to China's economy.

The Governor's Palace.

Beijing 's only concern was that no social democracy of the type so reviled under Soviet influence should be established on its doorstep. 'Those young officers frightened us with their ludicrous ideas', smiled Ho Yin, the owner of Tai Fung Bank and, more importantly, a 'Beijing man' in Macao, a few months after the event. 'The revolution can't be imported *a fortiori* to China', he continued with a mocking smile as he sipped his tea. We were on the terrace of his large house, a stone's throw from the Hotel Bela Vista. It dominated the Praia Grande, overlooking the Governor's residence. Mr Ho had begun his career as a money-changer in the streets of Canton (today known as Guangzhou) before moving to Macao. He'd knocked about a bit, sometimes navigating troubled waters during the war. But since the 1960s no one did anything in the 'Chinese territory under Portuguese administration' without the approval of this powerful banker, president of the Chinese Chamber of Commerce and a member of the People's Consultative Assembly. Portugal had changed its face but not its politics – it didn't have the initiative on that front. Macao remained Portuguese because China had decided that it should, lending

17

credence to the saying doing the rounds in town at the time: 'When Beijing sneezes Macao trembles, but it carries on dozing when Lisbon roars.' The two sentries with submachine-guns posted in front of the Governor's Pink Palace looked as bored as ever, until, as the handover drew near, a flow of important Portuguese civil servants sweeping past in official cars forced them to present arms more frequently. But the bureaucratic fever pitch of the handover didn't really make any impression on the operetta that was the enclave's Portuguese administration. The authorities removed the statue of Governor João Maria Ferreira do Amaral, which used to occupy pride of place in front of the Hotel Casino Lisboa, so as not to offend the Chinese. They say that this staunch patriot, who lost an arm in battle in Brazil and governed Macao from 1846 to 1849, had the unfortunate habit of horsewhipping recalcitrant Chinese. He was killed in an ambush. His severed head and amputated hand were carried in triumph to Canton. In the early 1990s Beijing let it be known that this 'unacceptable symbol of colonialism' had to be removed. And it duly was.

Today, a hotel built with Chinese capital from Beijing stands in place of Ho Yin's house. But his son, Edmund Ho, was made the first Chief Executive of the Macao S.A.R. after the handover. At least there is some continuity in Macao . . .

My train of thought is interrupted by the clinking sound of a cup of tea being brought to me by a waiter. The sun that rose above the Lisboa is already high in the sky. I'd allowed myself to drift through lingering images of memory lane, with my gaze lost in a Praia Grande still steeped in the uncertainty of dawn. But Macao's bewitching dawns are also a bitter experience. From the terrace of the Bela Vista, you can assess the disaster by averting your gaze ever so slightly from the narrow opening between Barra Hill and the sea. Bela Vista: the name no longer means much. The magnificent bay of the Praia Grande, with its succession of graceful curves and permanently low tides, where night fishermen used to lower large

Bela Vista Hotel, 1908.

traps held together by bamboo poles, has now been partially reclaimed to create two basins; a concrete tower taller than the Eiffel Tower will soon rise up on the reclaimed land, together with other buildings and hoardings. The bay itself is barricaded by a motorway . . . The ancient Indian fig trees that used to line the shore along that exquisite promenade, shaking their aerial roots like the hair of a person drowning, have been abandoned by soft verges dividing the new urban clearway that straightens the curve of the bay. Marooned amid asphalt, these trees offer a snapshot of the distressing shipwreck that used to be the 'blessed' Macao. Some cities are famous for their parks, others for their lovers' walks or sea views; the Praia Grande combined the best of everything a city can offer, wrote Shann Davies. Everything, or almost everything, has been swept aside, with the exception of a few hundred metres. The oleanders in the Bela Vista's garden have grown sufficiently to form a discreet screen blocking the view that has now been destroyed.

More than just a hotel, the Bela Vista was one of those romantic places that seemed untouched by time. Before being renovated in 1992, it was a charmingly old-fashioned establishment: Macao's soul incarnate, a sort of metaphor for the city. Built high up in colonial style with large verandahs, this two-storey building dominated the Praia Grande. People went there to enjoy the sunrise, or to admire the moon reflected in the waters of the China Sea of an evening. You ran into *aficionados* of Macao in the bar, like the tall, white-haired writer Austin Coates, who was both quintessentially British and very rude about his compatriots. Having fled Hong Kong, where he'd been based for many years, he went on to write several books relaxing on the Bela Vista's terrace.

The Bela Vista was a legend, at least to him. It was at the end of the 19th century that a British couple – Edward Clarke, who was captain of a ship that sailed the delta, and his wife, Catherine – decided to turn the attractive house overlooking the bay into a hotel. They called it Boa Vista. But after a few years they had to put it up for sale again. The hotel nearly became a sanatorium for French soldiers from Indo-China. There had already been a military hospital run by the Sisters of St Vincent de Paul, who nursed French soldiers wounded in China, in the parish of São Lourenço in 1858. But the game of alliances decided differently: the British, fearing an increased French influence in Macao, opposed the transfer. Lisbon conceded, and the hotel remained without a buyer. It then passed into the hands of the Santa Casa de Misericórdia before twice changing owners and subsequently becoming a hotel again, with first a French and then a British manager (who was chased out of the enclave when the police rumbled the clandestine roulette parties he was holding there). After a stint as a secondary school, it reverted to a hotel once again in 1936, this time under the name of Bela Vista. Far from the War, Macao played at being an ephemeral Bohemia. One year later, after the

The Bela Vista Hotel.

Japanese had invaded China, the hotel was requisitioned to welcome Portuguese refugees driven out of Shanghai. In 1958 it fell into the hands of three Chinese ladies, who turned it back into a hotel. Business was rarely prosperous and, to make matters worse, its manager Paulo Chung disappeared during the Cultural Revolution. He was succeeded by a colourful character, Adrião Pinto Marques. A great admirer of Napoleon and an indefatigable raconteur, Marques played his part in making the legend of the Bela Vista live again. He died peacefully in his armchair on the verandah. His Bela Vista, laden with Napoleonic souvenirs (ashtrays, busts, portraits and postcards of the Emperor), had an old-fashioned charm.

Because the hotel was situated on top of a small hill, rickshaw drivers with sweating torsos and muscular legs would invariably stop at the foot of the slope, turning on their saddles to gesture feebly towards the building. And so you continued on foot, reaching the hotel by climbing a *calçada* too steep for a rickshaw. The waiters looked as old as the building itself, and under as little pressure as the water in the bathroom pipes. But this decrepit hotel, with its spiral staircase and steps that cracked underfoot, its smell of mould during the rainy season and wheezy fans hanging from the ceiling to caress the warm night air, exuded the serene charm of old ladies of experience who have learned not to lie about their age.

The old Bela Vista closed in 1990. Tastefully restored by Bruno Suares and Irène O, two architects from Macao who endeavoured to preserve its ethos, the new Bela Vista has undoubtedly remained a privileged place: one of those luxury hotels as refined as its rooms are few and whose name figures alongside those other legendary Asian establishments (The Mandarin in Hong Kong, The Oriental in Bangkok, Raffles in Singapore, the Manila in Manila). 'We designed it as a dream, a folly', said Irène O. But despite the way the curtains in the huge bedrooms flapped in the breeze and the badly fitting windows let in torrents of rain during the typhoon season, the dusty old Bela Vista haunts the memories of those who spent time there.

The Bela Vista *was* Macao. When it closed for good, another page was ripped from the city's history.

My tea has grown cold. It is broad daylight now. These memories linger stubbornly in the glare . . . The prayer composed by Gerald Jollye – a subaltern in the British Army who was killed in 1950 in the Malayan jungle – in a poem written while he was staying at the Bela Vista, has not been answered: 'Let no one ever harm Macao.'

Macao from Penha Hill.

Macao Moments

What could you possibly want from today's unrecognizable Macao, where nothing is, only used to be, other than to re-familiarize yourself with the vanished images of a bygone era and find a setting for your daydreams among figments of memory and illusion? Torpid Macao at siesta time, well versed in inertia, its houses with their secretive shutters half-closed, its rickshaw drivers flopped on the back-seat with their feet up on the saddle. Macao of dazzling afternoons in dark streets where the sun plays hide-and-seek, furtively splashing pools of light while the sounds of shouting and women's laughter, interspersed with the clatter of mah-jong tiles being shaken, come drifting through doors made of wire-mesh to let in the cool air. Macao of typhoons, where, high up in the Chinese town behind Villa Camões, tropical downpours transform alleys of corrugated iron shacks into mud torrents. Grey-clad Macao, when the sticky sweat of the rainy season saturates everything, turning bodies limp, muffling street noises. Macao of smells: of camphor wood from gloomy workshops belonging to dubious antiques dealers; of steaming bowls of soup gulped on street benches; the cocktail of aromas from apothecaries' potions; a light damp breeze conveying the perfume of rain-soaked plants. Macao of summer evenings when the sweltering heat of day begins to ease off, and you can savour the cool of the garden at São José church, with its hibiscuses in full bloom. Macao by night over towards the Inner Harbour, its streets reeking with the acrid stench of urine and kelp, its blind alleys lit by the flickering glow of tiny shrines; the warm dark of sultry nights when you stumble across couples enacting the terrible game of happiness over on the ramparts by Monte Forte. Macao at dawn near the Lisboa, when the pawnbrokers arrive for the day shift and size up your watch in a glance, making you an offer before you've had a chance to speak. Macao of caged birds hanging from the windows of houses around São Paulo church, singing in harmony with birds nesting in its stone façade. Macao of gardens, where warbling concerts of infinite variety are conducted to the patter of footsteps: birds in delicate bamboo cages, hanging from the branches of trees and furnished with fine-glazed porcelain feeding bowls compete in song, while their owners, old men sitting on benches below, discuss their merits, pausing suddenly, heads tilted and fingers raised to point out particularly melodious passages. Indolent Macao of silent, stifling afternoons spent sitting on the harbour parapet facing the exquisite chapel of St Francisco Xavier, with its pale yellow facade of white festoons and its azure blue door from Coloane island, whose pediment bears the ideogrammatic inscription 'The House of the Lord'. Only the gentle lapping of waves marks the passing of time here. If we are to recapture something of yesterday's Macao, we should start with Coloane's village square.

With its forests and inlets, Coloane remained just outside of 'progress' as long as it could. As if somehow out of reach. An obelisk in the shady square in front of the chapel commemorates the defeat in 1910 of the last pirates. The island was one of their hideouts. In fact, the *ladrones*, as the Portuguese called them, persisted in their wicked ways under the leadership of a woman, Lai Choi San, a legendary character in the spirit of a female Robin Hood. This Queen of Pirates had inherited a flotilla of twelve junks equipped with old cannon from her buccaneering father, and during the 1920s she protected Macao's fisheries by imposing her law on the high seas with the tacit consent of the authorities. A blend of old Portugal and a China that no longer exists, Coloane more than Taïpa – the enclave's other island which once had charm all its own (a delightful Carmelite Monastery in a square of crude cobblestones planted with enormous Indian fig trees is one of its remnants) but now bristles with buildings – was until recently the end of the world in Macao; a leper house was even opened there.

Before 1972 one reached the island the Chinese conceded in 1887 by boat: a crossing that took almost an hour if you counted the stop at Taïpa. The boat left from the harbour at the foot of the A-Ma Temple and you disembarked not far from another more modest temple dedicated to Tan Gong, patron of fishermen. Coloane village has now been taken over by so-called antiques dealers, and the island, now joined to Taïpa by a causeway, has fallen prey to tourist developments. But the village remains Chinese in the evenings and at dawn, when old women in the square surrender themselves to *tai-chi*'s slow battle with the shade while workers from the shipyard meet at the Fai Gei café, not far from the lopsided houses on stilts. Coloane preserved its beaten earth alleys longer than most. On Rua dos Negociantes there used to be a shop belonging to the apothecary Ho Choi Song, his pharmacopoeia of aphrodisiacs lined up in jars under the altar on the wall with incense sticks burning in front of it. He's vanished. But in the square's public garden planted with palm trees there is still a Mediterranean

Coloane village.

bronze fountain with a cherubim and lion heads. Once, down the maze of alleys, you'd reach a tiny bistro with a regular clientèle. Vinho verde and warm bread would appear on your waxed tablecloth, followed by spicy dishes combining all the flavours Portugal had gleaned from across the world. Saludes, the Macanese owner, had the face of a freebooter and the big hands of a fighter. Chinese, Malay and Portuguese blood ran in his veins. When everyone had been served, he'd straddle a chair with his belly bulging, a fag end dangling from his lips, and with one eye on his audience he'd begin to spin yarns of his life as a sailor. On busy days he would even serve food in a sort of cubby-hole at the top of a narrow staircase where the ceiling sloped so low you could barely stand upright. Saludes has vanished, and his bistro with him. Gone too is the old beggar bundled in black rags who had his pitch for years on the restaurant terraces under the arcades in the square in front of the church, procuring crab carcasses with an imploring finger before sitting down in a wretched heap of tatters to gnaw them in a scrap of shade. Another Coloane character was the Italian Father Angelo Acquistapace, who for many years was guardian of the bones of Christian martyrs from Japan that had been laid to rest in the little chapel. The bones were displayed in cabinets lined with purple velvet, and were regularly dusted by the good Father. There was little love lost between him and the Communists, who had expelled him from China in 1949, and again in 1975 from Saigon, where he had run an orphanage. And so he came to Macao. After Mass, in front of an open door through which you can see the Chinese island of Dai Wan Kum on the other side of a narrow ribbon of sea, he would thunder *Vade retro, Satana!* Today, China has closed the gap, and the ribbon of water has been reduced through reclamation to a narrow channel. At the foot of hills, once forested but now disembowelled, rubbish skips appear out of the dust. Best to forget.

'Capri makes you forget everything', Lenin told Gorky when they stayed there at the beginning of the century – and it's true that Gorky had great difficulty leaving. Unlike that limestone rock off Naples, sun-grilled and pierced by the cries of cicada, Macao was never a fantasy magnet adrift from the world; no *must-see* for the cultural nomads of inter-war Europe on their rites-of-passage voyages; nor was it the romantic theatre of brief encounters, a utopian or chimerical refuge. But, in its own way, it knew how to make you forget everything. One of its charms lay in the fact that the city wasn't expecting anyone. It didn't give itself to you straightaway, like Italian cities do, intoxicating the eyes. It was a city of illusions, more bewitching than seductive. You discovered it step by step; it told its stories through leisurely strolls, encounters and whispered anecdotes. You'd be allowed to catch a brief, nonchalant glimpse, as of skin unexpectedly revealed when a piece of fabric slips.

With its hybrid of styles, Macao aroused a touching sense of wonder. Touching because its beauty was imperfect, and therefore human. It was carelessly beautiful. As artless as a face surprised on waking. Experts considered its architectural eclecticism to be clumsy: its models and references were ill-advised, and the wilful element of local culture was 'out of keeping'. But purism is not the issue here: the charm of this composite town where styles and eras habitually mingled lay precisely in the giant collage of lavish, and sometimes spectacularly bad, taste.

Arcaded streets, the faded splendour of houses in colonial or neo-classical styles with moulded façades; Hispanic-Moorish influences; wrought-iron balconies, balusters, fluted columns, pediments and cornices, festoons and serrations embellishing the deep, narrow Chinese houses with their gloomy inner courtyards; stone spiral staircases; pagoda roofs with grey tiles and upturned eaves pinned to the skies; the stucco décor of churches; shady loggias and ceramic corridors that rang out underfoot . . . Macao possessed the beauty of an archipelago that, in a dazzling exchange between two cultures, left the passer-by intoxicated.

Of course, you could always try researching the city's history in its libraries. But that would prove to be a rather pointless exercise. Macao's archives have partly disappeared, through negligence (overlooked by a city where for a long time the most precious documents were, the journalist and historian João Guedes likes to joke, bills of exchange), or else eaten by termites. But also through misfortune: destroyed by typhoons or fires. The final insult was the 'defenestration' of manuscripts from the Senate archives by the Red Guard during the Cultural Revolution. Even so, you might want to linger in the sumptuous and peaceful Senado Library, with its gleaming parquet and collection of antique bound books – one of the most extraordinary in the Far East – arranged on dark wooden shelves divided by a mezzanine and stretching all the way to the ceiling. But Macao is, above all, a city of narratives – chronicles, diaries of voyages, personal memories – with all the truth and imagination they can offer. A frustrating prism for the historian, but small matter when 'you could smell the history here' (Tiziano Terzani): a smell worth more than any book.

Macao was a place steeped in memory without ever becoming a repository: the present incorporated the past. A Braudélian past made from 'motion and stillness'. The enclave told a 'discreet history, almost undetected by its witnesses and actors, and withstanding the stubborn test of time'. Macao enjoyed the privilege of juxtaposing past and present until they were indistinguishable. And the past so successfully contaminated the present that an era without boundaries seemed to spread before you. To the charm of time standing still, Macao added that of accepting its decadence with good grace. Like Naples or Palermo, it was a city so lazily indifferent to its faded glory it exuded a calm lasciviousness in decline.

Macao survived until the early 1970s as a serenely decadent and gentle city, and this is how it was depicted by early 19th-century artists such as the British painter George Chinnery (1774–1852), who spent the last 27 years of his life there, and the Frenchman Auguste Borget (1808–77). Borget only stayed six months, between 1838 and 1839, but his depictions of the city, published in *China and the Chinese* in 1842, rank among the best

The Praia Grande from the East by George Chinnery.

works of this little known artist. Chinnery left pastel or ink sketches, as well as watercolours and large-scale oil paintings: the art historian César Guillen-Nuñez likens his sketches to Rembrandt, his Macao and mainland *vedute* to painters of the Venetian school, and his portraits to Velásquez or Sir Thomas Lawrence.

An outmoded world? Not really. For these artists had the distinction of being attached to the dust of everyday life, to an intimate, anonymously human Macao: the Macao of the streets and its people. Aside from his commissioned portraits, which had their own appeal (such as the fine *Chinese Lady With Fan*), Chinnery depicted fishermen and boatmen, barbers, porters, peasants, coolies staggering beneath planks of timber, crouching gamblers, craftsmen in wrought iron, pedlars, women with children on their backs . . . Blending Neoclassical and Romantic styles in his sketchbooks, these drawings and rough impressions from the life afford an ethnological dimension to the work of this 'observer of human nature'. Chinnery clearly made the aesthetic decision to 'unleash the poetry of prose', affording his depictions of Macao a somewhat idealized

São Lourenço church.

character. As we will see, the Macao of his era was also tragic. But the gentle Macao he paints (as did other artists after him, from Borget to Maciano Baptista, a Macanese painter in the second half of the 19th century, or, later still, in the mid-20th, the Russian George Smirnoff) represents one of this city's many true faces.

The difference between Macao today and the city depicted by these artists (irreversible damage aside) lies in the swarming bustle of life as compared to the sleepy village atmosphere that emerges from their works. But the images bequeathed to us in Chinnery's and Borget's works still confront the stroller wandering through places they recorded more than a century ago, from São Lourenço church down towards the Praia Grande, from São Domingos via A-ma's Temple, the 'bazaar' (impressively evoked by Borget) to the Inner Harbour.

Even in those days an invisible line already divided Macao, from Barra Hill in the south-west all the way to the imposing citadel of Monte Forte in the north-east via the Largo do Senado, forming a triangular public square in the city's centre: the Christian town spread out to the east; the Chinese town to the west. Let us wander through the latter's maze.

George Chinnery used to live a stone's throw away from São Lourenço church, where the border between the two Macaos cuts the ridge of his hill. A street was named after him in 1974, to commemorate the 200th anniversary of his birth. To the right, the street gives onto the Rua Ignazio Baptista, where Chinnery's house (now replaced by an apartment block) used to be. Today there's a McDonald's on the corner. The street drops sharply for 30 metres or so before levelling off at right-angles to the Rua do Bazarinho (Little Market Street). Anonymous apartment blocks six or seven storeys high cramp the street, their balconies bristling with bamboo poles that support the washing hung out to dry like banners above the heads of passers-by, while down at ground level there are repair workshops and an electrical goods store. On the corner with the Rua Casa Forte, a few metres along on the left, the fruit sellers sit. At the turn, in front of a modest shrine covered with smoke-blackened vermilion ceramic tiles, sticks of incense burn in honour of the local divinity. Attached to the tips of the altar roof, more incense burns slowly in huge tapering spirals. Two oil-lamps diffuse a flickering glow. Women barely pause on their way past, as they light a stick of incense, bow their heads and make *wai*. The festival of the Divinity of Place (*Tu Di*) occurs on the first day of the second lunar month (towards mid-March). The shrine is decorated with flowers and offerings (fruits and bowls of rice), and trestle tables are set up in the street. In the evening the residents sit at these tables eating glazed suckling pigs.

Wherever you amble through these little streets, you come across tiny shrines dedicated to a local divinity: a plain stone daubed with red at the foot of a house, a recess in a wall, or modest iron boxes fixed at head-height containing 'bundles' of incense sticks. These little shrines are surmounted by a rectangular plaque bearing four large golden ideograms to identify the object of worship. These subordinates of the 'Divinities of Walls and Ditches' are the appointed protectors of a domain – a district, or block of houses. They are supplicated in order to grant wealth, peace and happiness to the neighbourhood, and deaths are announced to them. Strips of red paper with large golden ideograms hang from the top of nearly every door: these are good-luck charms for whomever crosses the threshold. Macao has remained an extraordinary living museum of ancient Chinese traditions and beliefs.

The bliss of the Asian street, where intimacy blends with collective life, is recaptured in Macao. A street is everything at once: it is a market, a kitchen, a place where you can rest or take a siesta on a litter at the end of an alley or sit on a chair and read your newspaper in the evening cool, a forum for neighbourhood gossip, a children's playground, the overspill of a shop or workshop. Horns blare as motorbikes push through the small crowd of neighbours getting ready for the Festival of the Rua do Bazarinho. Unperturbed by all this excitement, an old man in a cap and jacket with a frayed Mao collar of washed-out grey shuffles along with a walking stick in one hand and a small bamboo cage in the other: a piece of material half-covers the chirping bird inside.

The Rua do Bazarinho continues a few dozen metres before becoming an alley, with more fruitsellers encamped on the same asphalt. To the left is the Patio da Ilasão with its brick arch pierced by a small window, and then, after a turn to the right, the Travessa do Abreu takes you back towards the Rua Padre Antonio and the sound of traffic.

Not far from here, the small square known as the Largo do Lilau used to be a peaceful haven, but traffic got the better of it. The low-level houses bordering it have been restored. Their fronts, which once looked leprous, have now been repainted in attractive pastel shades: sand yellow, pale green, and over there old-fashioned pink. At dawn, a few old women slowly practise their stretching exercises, slapping their legs from time to time beneath an enormous Indian fig tree. Through a half-open window, you can see the red light-bulbs of a shrine. Heading down towards the Inner Harbour by the narrow Travessa Antonio da Silva, you stumble on a porch to your left. This leads into a small courtyard hidden by the wall of the house in front of you. The red and green altar beneath the portico is adorned only with a few slender sticks of incense. Three steps lead down past a recess to a rectangular courtyard below, where stone benches flank the dull brick walls surmounted by green ceramic cornices. At the far end, another gate opens onto a second narrow courtyard, where washing is hung out to dry on long bamboo poles. Large ideograms on a faded wooden plaque bear the name of a transport company. With one or two exceptions, the houses here are uninhabited. They are in varying states of decay: their windows have been ripped out, lop-sided doors are closed with rusty chains and padlocks. The creeper that cascades over the rooftops, abundantly in places, tells the story of neglect. Two small, narrow courtyards in shadow are now the kingdoms of cats, stretched out lazily on the cool paving. If you

Baroque and modern in old Macao.

crane your neck, you can sometimes see inside the houses and glimpse sections of translucent walls made from tiny mother-of-pearl tiles and mounted on a wooden trellis, giving the room the diaphanous light that is special to the few houses in Macao that have retained such features.

If you continue down the Travessa Antonio da Silva, you pass women slowly climbing back up the slope carrying heavy plastic bags filled with groceries. The commotion from the market in Rua Praia do Manduco rises distinctly now from the streets below. And, unexpectedly, you are surrounded by stalls disappearing under piles of fruit, vegetables, meat, underwear, clothes and garish multi-coloured gilt bundles of incense reflecting the sunlight. Carried along by the throng, you advance between the trestle tables and rickety stools of street dives producing all kinds of food. Activities, smells and noises mix and mingle. There's the smell of victuals, the waft of soup, the whiff of algae and dried fish with gaping gills, all lined up or hung by the tail. People sniff, look, barter, buy and sell. Customers are solicited by smooth talking while cooks prepare their food. It is always time to eat in the Chinese quarter, particularly for the Cantonese. They chop and trim, slice and carve, plunge handfuls of noodles into boiling water or toss them into deep black woks. There are mountains of soya in cooking basins, chickens whose pallid skins glisten with grease, coppery ducks hanging from hooks and roasted suckling pigs laid out in a final parade on a box decorated with pink ribbon; doughnuts sizzle next to Portuguese delicacies, steamed meat patties, every kind of dried fruit and shellfish, huge pale shark fins wrapped in plastic, and sinister snakes with parchment skin coiled into bottles.

This 'gastronomy of the eye', so dear to Balzac, used to continue inside the São Lourenço covered market, which has since been transformed. The sickly smell of blood once hung over the place. There were whole districts of pork meat, bundles of tripe and fish of every kind and size twitching in the water at the bottom of long zinc vats. The thrusting crowd in front of the stalls would part suddenly to let through deliverymen carrying twelve chickens or ducks strung up by their ankles, thrusting their heads up to warble their despair in vain. They would be dispatched on the spot and dressed immediately. With the exception of fish, all this market produce came from China. A fact that Beijing never missed a chance to remind the Portuguese.

The fortune-teller in the Leal Senado Square in front of the Casa Misericórdia seemed impervious to change. He'd been there for years. The two of us would exchange a few friendly words of recognition as we traced the ideograms on my note-

Street scenes in old Macao.

book in silence – the only way of communicating for someone who doesn't speak Chinese. There is a small temple in a hidden recess of the street that runs alongside São Domingos and adjoins the covered market. It is among the oldest (built in 1750), and one of only a few of relative importance built in the centre of town. It's dedicated to Guan Di, patron of loyalty, who is ready to intervene against those who trouble the people's peace. Wreathed in curls of incense, it appears from the outside to be as dark as entrails kindled by the red glow of the altar lights. When a visitor enters, three neon lights suddenly glare over the carved wooden altar. The future is predicted here, and geomancy is practised in order to determine the best alignment for a house or business (a gauge of its prosperity) together with the art of physiognomy, in which a person's character (a future spouse, for example) can be discerned from the form of his or her face. Time-honoured Chinese beliefs remain anchored in the imaginations of Macao's citizens. No construction work is undertaken, from the Hotel Casino Lisboa down, without conforming to the rules of geomancy.

The temple of Guan Di also accommodates the association of Three Streets – or two, as they really are now: Rua Ervanários (the Street of Herbalists) and Rua das Estalagens (the Street of Businesses), the main commercial street in the Chinese district of Ou-Mun. The temples don't just have a religious function: they're also the focal points of a district's social life.

In the web of streets and alleys (Travessa dos Mercados, Travessa Alfaitas, Rua Camílio Pessanha, Travessa do Pagode . . .), there's a succession of small businesses in shacks mostly open to the four winds: a locksmith's, a haberdasher's, a tailor's, a wood-carver's; the back of a restaurant where crouching women chop up vegetables and wash chickens in large bowls of blood-stained water; an ironmonger's full of bric-à-brac; sellers of every kind of incense (still produced in significant quantities in Macao, as were fireworks on the island of Taïpa until the early 1960s); a carpenter's workshop where altars are crafted; birdcage-makers; a typographer; a hairdresser-cum-earcleaner with a simple

A typical Macao street scene.

awning of rusty corrugated iron over his armchair; a dealer in religious objects and golden buddhas; an ivory carver in front of his lathe; apothecaries lining up their bottles of mysterious substances with smells you can only guess at; second-hand goods dealers like old Teng Weng, whose shop has been in his family for three generations and whose dusty treasure hoard, consisting exclusively of objects from Macao, occupies three floors reached at your peril by climbing a rickety staircase. A huge alabaster statue of the Virgin Mary by the door stands next to one of Guan Di, whose dimensions are no less impressive.

Most of the signs are in Portuguese and Chinese. Even for a *'mestre de medicina chinesa'*. It was in the district of the Inner Harbour, around the old temple of Hong Kung Miu with its decrepit paintwork, to the western end of the Rua das Estalagens, and along the Largo do Pagode do Bazar, that the Chinese town sprang up. Before the causeways were built in the late 1890s, the Largo do Pagode do Bazar followed the sea. And the area's streets are still curved from the days when they hugged the shape of the Praia Manduco. You can still find the oldest apothecaries in this district of leprous-looking houses, and as you walk past their shops you'll hear the sound of pestle and mortar reducing plants into a powder that is weighed in a set of copper scales hanging from a beam. In the Travessa do Auto Novo, Chá Medicinal Un Iec, an old herbalist who specializes in all sorts of teas with multiple properties has been keeping shop for a century. In some places bamboo scaffolding props up a wall on the verge of collapse or forces apart two sides of an alley stubbornly leaning inwards. This is also the district of Cantonese restaurants and stalls whose traders use tongs to grill fine rectangular slivers of dried meat. When night falls, the district twinkles with signs. But the further north you head in the direction of the border with China – formerly a gate closed at nightfall, like that of a medieval town – the poorer and more mundane the area as it becomes another 'developed' Chinese town: mass-living, traffic jams, garish advertisements, straight dirty roads, half-built apartment blocks, workshops and factories. Yet behind the Camões Garden lies an old, poor Chinese district that has hardly changed at all with the passing years, one full of straight alleys and houses patched up with pieces of rusty sheet metal. In the course of these little streets you arrive back at the Temple of the Sleeping Buddha (Tai Soi Miu), with its maze of small rooms and corridors, and its army of beggars.

Time to draw breath. Perhaps at Hong Kung Miu, where an offering is always worth a mouthful of tea served in a minuscule cup, or else, as in the old days, at the ancient Lok Kok tea house on the Rua de Cinco de Outubro, an old street in the district of the Inner Harbour. Its rooms spread over two floors were always packed and buzzing, ringing with the sound of raised voices bouncing off the green ceramic walls decorated with large mirrors. The Lok Kok, where once one could meet sailors and gamblers from the floating casino at dawn, closed in 1994. But in the same street the Kun Nam Casa de Chá, with its tinny music and sign displaying a coiled dragon on high, has kept going.

Is Macao a *Chinese* city? Only up to a point. For Macao was never really Chinese, or European. Like Shanghai, it was always a city *in* China. And yet China is there: 'The air is in some way saturated with China, and physically continues to invade us, even in our most intimate thoughts and activities', wrote the French diplomat Théophile de Ferrière Le Vayer back in the 1850s. And still today, despite the marks left by Europe, China envelops you, breathes you in. But it is a China you'd have difficulty finding today, even in China itself.

Drowsy Macao has been more successful than hectic Hong Kong in preserving ancestral ways of life and products banned under the Communists. Unlike Shanghai, where two cities – one European and the other Chinese – stood side by side without merging, or Hong Kong's jungle of millionaires, white-collar workers and down-and-outs, where foreigners led one life and the Chinese another (only money partially bridged these divides), Macao always took the blending of residents and customs further. Perhaps because Hong Kong's land was merely borrowed and thus the clock was always ticking, many there were always reckoning on one day packing up and going. But throughout its history, and for the British just as for the Chinese, Hong Kong remained primarily a *colony* and never an adopted land or a refuge – apart from for those fleeing Communist China. Because Macao's ambiguous status was in the interests of both Lisbon and Beijing and the 'colonists' wasted so little time colonizing, the osmosis that took place was more pronounced, translating into a multi-racial culture that was shaped with the passing centuries by the need to co-exist. But there was one exception: faiths. These lived on, side by side, without ever contaminating one other: rites and festivals were preserved while, like sentinels, the respective figures of devotion and protection in the form of temple divinities and church saints sketched out the city's spiritual topography. This labyrinth of piety created intersecting and overlapping 'territories' whose 'boundaries' are invisible to an outsider but well known to the local inhabitants, as the historian Jonathan Porter noticed.

Macao's unique character used to lie in the confluence of two cultures, as well as in the implicit recognition of their incompatibilities: a beacon in the history of tolerance. But how did this cultural precipitate, now in the process of dissolving, form in the first place? It is time to tell the tale of this city.

Across the roofs to the castle in the distance.

The Cross, Spices and 'White Metal'

There's a small Mediterranean plaza at the top of the rise, paved in black and white with an ancient and imposing Indian fig tree in the middle. You get to it from the Rua Central, climbing a few paces back up the slope from the Calçada do Teatro. On your way, you'll see the delightful Dom Pedro V Theatre: a small, pale green neo-classical building with white mouldings and one side facing the plain west front of Santo Agostinho Church; and then you're in this *'piazzetta'* on Asian soil. To the left of the theatre lies the entrance to the Seminário de São José; there's an attractive house with faded yellow walls and white moulding straight ahead, now the Sir Robert Ho Tung Library: the fabulously wealthy Hong Kong businessman, knighted by the British crown in the early stages of the 20th century, donated his summer home and book collection to the city. The approach is through a small garden where frangipani scents the air. Another walled garden on the other side of the house is a blur of shaded patio and pergolas. Returning under the green hydra of the Indian fig tree in the *piazzetta* and keeping right of Santo Agostinho Church, you'll reach the gate to the residence of the Jesuit fathers, Vila Flor.

Heading back down the Calçada do Gambao in the opposite direction from the Rua Central, you quickly find yourself in the maze of tiny streets that make up the old Chinese town. By contrast, the Praia Grande side of the hill was once the shining heart of the Portuguese town, where the beautiful houses of wealthy merchants sprawled all the way to the bay, flanked by two citadels on the hills of Barra, to the south, and Guia, to the north. The *piazzetta*, the highest point of this invisible line separating the Christian town from the Chinese town, forms (together with the São Paulo church) a twin heart to the 'City in the Name of God in China' (*Cidade do Nome de Deus na China*) that was Macao.

Each trip entailed an obligatory visit to the São José Seminary, down long vaulted corridors whose flagstones rang with the sound of footsteps, to meet Father (now Monsignor) Manuel Teixeira. Established by Jesuits in 1728 as a joint foundation with the São Paulo College, this huge residence was all but deserted when the Church recalled its seminarians to Portugal and Hong Kong, for fear the Cultural Revolution would spread to Macao. They never came back. Up in his attic study, surrounded by piles of annotated books towering up from the floor and heaps of papers and newspapers collapsing over tables and chairs, Mgr Teixeira proved a generous raconteur who would talk about Macao for hours on end, occasionally taking his lucky visitor to see some spot he'd been describing. The author of 130 books and brochures about the city and its surrounding region, including an impressive history of the Church in sixteen volumes, his white Dominican cassock and beard were a familiar sight in the streets of Macao. More than anyone else, he personifies Macao's memory. He was twelve when he arrived in the enclave. It was customary at the time for priests to bring young seminarists back to the enclave from their rare trips to Portugal. Which is how the young Manuel (born in 1912) disembarked in Macao in the 1920s. For a long time, he was responsible for the parish of the elegantly peaceful neighbouring church, São Lourenço, with its turquoise ceiling and terracotta panelling (the work of Chinese artisans) integrated into the scheme of its interior décor. Palm-tree branches in the garden brush lightly against the pale yellow and white facade flanked by two neo-classical towers: together with the bell-tower of São Paulo, these were the first landmarks Macao offered the new arrival at a time when the city only boasted low-rise housing. Mgr Teixeira owes his passion for history to Father Jean-Francis-Régis

São José Seminary.

São José church.

Gervaix from the Overseas Missions in Paris, who taught French in the Seminary before being appointed to Beijing, and who in 1928 published *An Abridged History of Macao* in two volumes, under the pseudonym Eudore de Colomban. 'We can't stop anything. Or save anything,' said Mgr Teixeira, a few months prior to handover. 'But history at least must be preserved, and there'll still be books. I'm just the ghost of a vanished city.'

Down yet more vaulted corridors away from the seminary, past a charming walled garden planted with hibiscus, you'll find one of the most beautiful churches in Macao: São José. Also flanked by two towers and with that rare and original feature in China, a dome, this building displays a Baroque influence in the curve of its façade and in its interior. There's an unusual kind of relic venerated at São José: a humerus, belonging to Francisco Xavier. Hoping to the end for a return to China, this missionary responsible for India and Japan died virtually alone in December 1552 in a hut on the small island of Shanqian (Shangchuan) to the west of Macao. His corpse was laid to rest at Goa, and the right arm was amputated in 1619. One bone was sent to Japan, where the saint had begun his evangelizing mission. But persecution forced the Jesuits to flee the archipelago and seek refuge in Macao, bringing the relic with them. Another bone, from the apostle's forearm, is venerated at the Chiesa del Gesù in Rome. A third, sent to Cochin in India, was lost.

The Jesuits arrived in the enclave not long after the first navigators (in 1562, for example, in the case of Father Luis Frois, who took off again to preach the gospel in Japan). Throughout the first half of the 16th century, the maritime efforts of the Portuguese to break the Venetian monopoly on the spice trade, had led them round the Cape of Good Hope into the Indian Ocean. After seizing the port of Goa, on India's western coast, as the capital of their mercantile empire in 1510, they conquered the peninsula of Malacca the following year, reaching Timor and the Moluccas before heading back along the Chinese coast from 1513. Gold and silver from India, raw and brocaded silks from China, batik from Java, precious stones from Burma, camphor from Borneo, sandalwood from Timor, as well as peppers and spices: Lisbon's appetite (and beyond Portugal, that of Europe) was insatiable. But another profitable source had appeared: Japan.

The archipelago had been stumbled across accidentally towards 1543 by various buccaneers. Its discovery had been attributed, though not without some embellishing of the facts, to the adventurer and teller of tall tales Fernão Mendes Pinto, who was washed up by a storm on the coast of Tanegashima island (south of Kyûshu) in a Chinese smuggler's junk. The rapid development of trade with the archipelago that followed this discovery prompted the Portuguese to establish a depot in China.

Under the Ming dynasty China had closed itself off. Distrust of foreigners led to restrictions on external trade, particularly with Japan, and official relations between the two countries were virtually severed from 1549. But Beijing continued to encourage trade. And because social instability was widespread in an archipelago torn apart by feudal wars, Japanese piracy had become an endemic force of evil throughout Oriental Asia. The pirates (wâko), a Far-Eastern breed of Vikings, sowed terror along the Korean and Chinese coasts as far as the island of Hainan. As well as Japanese piracy, a form of Chinese piracy emerged. And, from the 1550s onwards, Sino-Japanese relations degenerated into savage exchanges.

The Portuguese seized the chance to become intermediaries between China and Japan, taking advantage of the Japanese demand for Chinese fabrics and raw silks paid for in silver from the archipelago's mines. At the time, Japan was a sort of Far-Eastern mini-Mexico with large numbers of active silver mines (particularly on the island of Sado, on the northwest coast). And so began the triangular pattern of Chinese–Japanese–Portuguese trade, along the route from Nagasaki to

Lisbon via Canton, Macao, Malacca and Goa. In spring, ships arrived from Goa loaded with Portuguese and Indian merchandise which was then traded for Chinese goods; taking advantage of the early summer monsoon, the ships would next head for Japan, returning with holds laden with 'white metal' (silver). The biennial Cantonese fair in January and June enabled the Portuguese to procure Chinese merchandise. Which is how 'the voyage to Japan' came to be the source of Macao's wealth, with the city enjoying a golden age between 1550 and 1650.

The Portuguese ruled the waters between India and Japan, using large ships equipped with cannons to drive out the pirates. They began looking for a port that would provide a permanent depot. After trying the islands of Shangchuan and Limapo (Zhejiang), they ventured into the labyrinth of islands in the Pearl river delta. They set up camp at the tip of the isthmus, near the mouth of the Pearl. The delta was an area rich in fish, due to the wealth of alluvial deposits brought down the river, and its coastline was dotted with fishing villages. Rarely had a location been more propitious for trade. Two transport systems converged in the delta: riverine and maritime. Products from the Chinese interior (tea, silk, minerals and porcelain) arrived via the Pearl river. Beyond the narrow waters, the ocean beckoned. 'All of Macao's wealth is in the sea, and the whole city lives off it. The only goods of any value are those brought by wind and tide; when they're in short supply, everything's in short supply', wrote Father Luis da Gama (a Jesuit inspector) with some justification in the mid-17th century.

But for a thin strip of land linking it to the mainland, the promontory where the Portuguese settled would have been an island. The place was called 'the waters reflected' (*haojing*) or just 'the bay' (*ao*) by its inhabitants, on account of two wide natural harbours to the east and west of the swollen section of the peninsula. But with several channels leading between the islands towards the open sea south of the isthmus, the area was also denoted by the phrase 'the gateway of the bays' (*aomen*). Towards the south-west was the small temple previously mentioned; built by a merchant from Fujian miraculously rescued in a storm, it was dedicated to A-Ma the Compassionate. When the first sailors reached Aomen and asked what the place was called, the fishermen told them they were in the 'Bay of A-Ma': *Amakou*, in the local dialect, which became Macau or Macao. In Chinese literature the place has kept the name of Aomen.

In 1553 the Guangdong authorities granted right of establishment to Leonel de Souza, captain of a seven-strong fleet of ships, in exchange for taxation and the levying of custom duties. Did this mean the Portuguese had obtained what amounted to a purely oral concession in return for their part in ridding the region of pirates? Their cannon had certainly proved effective. But was that the only reason? The financial benefits enjoyed by regional authorities accrued from trade were surely another. Either way, the concession was never sanctioned in writing and remained a tacit arrangement until the treaty of 1887, when China, weakened by the Opium Wars, recognised Portugal's 'perpetual occupation' of the territory. But Macao had already prospered from a shrewdly protracted misunderstanding for three centuries. As far as the Cantonese authorities were concerned, the 'barbarians' had been authorized to settle on a piece of territorial confetti in the far-flung reaches of the empire, for services rendered (their cannon had significantly helped quash a mutiny in 1563) and for the profits arising from their presence; they were not, in Chinese eyes, beneficiaries of any concession. For their part, the Portuguese believed right of sovereignty had been granted to them, and began building houses, warehouses and churches on their territory, as well as forts at each extremity of the Praia Grande. Some twenty years later, in 1573, the Chinese closed off the isthmus at its narrowest point with a high wall (at the top of the lotus flower 'stem' it formed), affording foreign presence on this strip of land a more durable character. A gate resembling that of a medieval citadel, normally open on market days, bore the ideogrammatic inscription: 'Fear our greatness and respect our virtue.'

So Macao was never conquered, nor was it a spoil of war wrenched from China as Hong Kong was to be by the British three centuries later. It preserved its ambiguous status. Lisbon never really considered the enclave a Lusitanian territory, any more than Beijing did. Unlike the Portuguese possessions in Asia, Macao was never properly speaking a 'colony'. Born from the initiative of merchant sailors and not some grand strategy dreamed up in Lisbon, the city enjoyed such a degree of autonomy it was known as the 'First Republic of the Orient'. The enclave was administered by its 'citizenry' according to collective law. From 1582, the merchant community equipped itself with the Senado da Câmera, an elected organ for administering civil affairs. It chose its own judges as well as a representative accredited to the local Chinese authorities. The costs of maintaining the garrison and the upkeep of the forts placed under the authority of a governor answerable to Goa (the capital of the Portuguese empire in Asia) were met by the city out of income arising from taxes levied on trading. The Senado also financed charitable organizations such as the Santa Casa de Misericórdia. Founded in 1569, and the second most important institution in the city, this fraternity invested the capital deposited with it or bequeathed to it by making loans to merchants as a stake in their maritime trading ventures.

Macao held onto its undefined status throughout its history: even after China had recognized the 'perpetual occupation' of the territory by Portugal in 1887, the question of sovereignty was never clear-cut. The enclave's ambiguous status afforded its inhabitants a feeling of independence from both Portugal and China.

The Italian Jesuit Alessandro Valignano, successor to Francisco Xavier in the business of evangelizing Japan and China, would have us believe that China conceding Macao was the 'fruit' of the apostle's prayers. Certainly, both the enclave and the missions enjoyed untold wealth for a whole century.

The Portuguese are often depicted as blazing a trail towards the East in search of 'spices and souls', with a sabre in one hand and a Bible in the other. But it was trade that primarily attracted the first *conquistadores*: Macao's merchant adventurers were not so much conquerors as traders looking for anchorages from which they could do business. Propagating the faith seems initially to have been more of an embarrassment than an asset for such pragmatic men. These Portuguese versions of 'Volpone' could be construed, for example, as deeming it impolitic to assist Xavier in his voyage to China at a time when they were involved in laborious negotiations with the Chinese about their settlement of the delta; these nomads of the seas preferred instead to leave the evangelizer dejected and dying on his island. Subsequently, the missions were officially associated with expanding trade: thanks to a papal bull from Gregory XIII (1576), those nicknamed the 'pepper crusaders' benefited from the patronage (*padroado*) of the King of Portugal: in other words, they were charged with the same duties and afforded the same privileges as the Church back home, which was supported and protected by the Crown. The first Bishop of Macao was responsible for China and the Japanese islands. From that moment on, trade and mission were closely linked, and the refusal of the Macao authorities to renounce their programme of evangelization contributed to the Tokugawa's decision to close off the country to everyone except the Dutch, who weren't fired with the same proselytizing zeal.

While the Franciscans ruled over 'Spanish' Manila (the Philippines had become a colony of Madrid in the early 1500s), the Jesuits 'appropriated' the 'Portuguese' Macao, at least until the mid-18th century when they were chased out by the despotic Marquis of Pombal, who dissolved their order by decree.

Supported by the King of Portugal and granted extensive privileges to propagate the faith in Asia, the Jesuits originally concentrated their evangelizing efforts on Japan, where the prospects seemed more hopeful. Xavier went from Goa, the capital of the Portuguese mercantile empire where he had arrived in 1542, to Malacca. There he met a Japanese called Anjiro in 1547, a native of Kagoshima and probably a petty Samurai who'd fled the archipelago on account of some dirty deed. His tales amazed the apostle, who decided to head for the archipelago without delay. Disappointed by India, Xavier had now begun pinning his main hopes on Japan. He set out two years later and stayed there 30 months, laying the foundation stone of evangelization: Japan's 'Christian century' had begun. But Xavier was disappointed by his welcome from the authorities (the Emperor refused to receive him), and he left the archipelago in 1551 with the conviction that the process of evangelization had to begin in China, and the insight that the Portuguese had to speak the language of the natives as well as understand their thought processes, in order to convert them.

Xavier wasn't insensitive to cultural differences. But he was driven by a fervent faith, and tended to think that for Divine Providence to be revealed to them, it was enough to 'disabuse' the 'infidels' and proclaim: 'Pray to God, good people!' His evangelical enthusiasm enabled him to communicate with the poorest in society, but just as his oratorical spats with the Japanese bonzes had taught him a bitter lesson, so he came up against stiff resistance as soon as he encountered the Mandarins. Xavier's intuitions would inform a fresh approach to missionary action in Japan and China as elaborated by his successors, and in particular by the Italian Jesuit Father Alessandro Valignano, who arrived in Macao in 1557 as Visitor General of the Society of Jesus. His domain extended from the Ganges all the way to the furthest outpost of the Orient.

Valignano decided to adopt a different approach to missionary action, changing the evangelizing 'strategy' by practising what he referred to as '*il modo soave*'. This meant learning the language, both for practical reasons and for a better understanding of the culture of those countries where the gospel was to be spread. And so it was with this aim of adapting to societies and civilizations as different as those of China and Japan, that Valignano inaugurated what would later come to be known as 'inculturation': a process whereby, instead of alienating new converts from their environment by seeking to 'Europeanize' them, foreigners were offered a Christian message adapted to their own cultural context.

Despite 30 years' work by the Jesuit Luis Frois (who arrived a little after Xavier, in 1563) exploring the customs and local culture in Japan – his *Treaty on the Contradictions between European and Japanese Customs* is one of the best accounts of the country at the time – the practice of 'brutal' evangelization towards the Japanese shocked Valignano. Like Luis Frois, he was struck by how radically different the Japanese were, and, in the course of three trips to the archipelago and in his *Summary of Matters Concerning the Province of Japan and its Government* (1583), he formulated directives to the Fathers and Brothers of missions in Japan recommending they adapt to local habits. The new 'policy' of evangelization that was supposed to develop in China was therefore inaugurated in Japan, but it was in Macao that it was most widely practised.

This approach was not easily accepted by many members of the Society of Jesus. It must have paid off, however, since the number of Christians rose from 215,000 in 1590 to 400,000 by the beginning of the next century. But Christianity's spectacular progress in the archipelago was stopped dead in its tracks: Toyotomi Hideyoshi, the second of the country's three great unifiers, was initially tolerant of but later irritated by relations between the missionaries and the lords from the south of the archipelago. In 1587 he forbade the lords to convert and ordered the expulsion of the missionaries. This measure was partially enforced. Ten years later the first persecutions began, (26 Christians, including six Franciscan and three Japanese Jesuits, were martyred). They continued into the next century and culminated in the edict of 1613 proscribing Christianity:

Japan's 'Christian century' ended when the Shimabara (Kyûshû) insurrection was crushed in 1637. The country's rulers seem to have feared the growth of a religion pernicious to the social order and causing unrest, as had been the case with the Leagues of the Faithful from Buddhist sects a century before. The close-knit relationship between trade and mission in Japanese ports, combined with Macao's refusal to renounce the process of evangelization, seem eventually, as we've seen, to have influenced the Tokugawa's decision to close the archipelago to foreigners.

Persecuted, and crushed in the Battle of Shimabara, the Japanese Christians were forced to recant their faith before being dispersed throughout the country. Some pursued a clandestine form of worship in the islands off Nagasaki, without priest or sacrament. Others fled to Macao just before the archipelago was sealed off in 1635. Among them were artisans and artists who went on to contribute to the blossoming of the arts in the Portuguese enclave: one painting, a naïve depiction of the martyrdom of the Nagasaki Christians (identified by name on the canvas), dated 1597, is attributed to an anonymous Franciscan father and kept in the São José Seminary. And it was to Macao that the bones of 59 martyrs were brought by Japanese fleeing the persecutions; they were laid to rest at São Paulo church and then at the small chapel of São Francisco on the island of Coloane before being returned to Japan in 1991.

Valignano's spell in Japan convinced him as to the merits of Francisco Xavier's view: spreading the gospel in China was the greatest priority of all, even if it seemed as unrealistic as an 'impresa desperata'. And Macao became the 'laboratory' where he implemented this new strategy with two other Italian Jesuits, Michele Ruggieri and Matteo Ricci, the latter a remarkable craftsman.

The Jesuits arrived in Macao in 1565, and established their presence within a few decades by building the St Martin Oratory and their first college, completed in 1594. Rebuilt after a fire, the Madre de Deus College, next door to the lavish São Paulo church, became the most prestigious institution in Asia on account of its printing press and library of 4,200 books. Generations of missionaries were educated at the first Western university in Asia to teach all the sciences offered by Europe's great academic institutions; and having braved the terrors of the sea, scurvy and attacks from pirates in order to reach Macao, they set off again to spread the word in China, Japan, Korea, Tonkin and Borneo. Franciscans and Dominicans as well as Jesuits passed through Macao, which became the 'Rome of the Far East' and the 'mother of missions in Asia'. Without this headquarters, Jesuit proselytizing in Japan and China in particular would have been impossible: Alessandro Valignano had shrewdly obtained permission from the Senado for the missions to receive a proportion of the profits from trade with Japan. Between 1578 and 1740, some 430 Jesuits set out from Lisbon for Macao.

Matteo Ricci landed in the Portuguese enclave in 1582, to complete preparations for his Chinese mission. A great mind versed in the Chinese classics and initiated in Buddhism and Taoism, Ricci dabbled in Western science in order to attract the attention of the Chinese elite. He stayed in Macao for a relatively short time, moving the following year to Zhaoqing, the administrative capital of Guangdong, with his predecessor Michel Ruggieri who had stayed in the enclave for two years. Then he set off again for Beijing.

It was also in Macao that the Jesuit Johann Adam Schall von Bell perfected his Chinese. This learned father's knowledge of astronomy so fascinated the Chinese that in 1644 they made him the first foreign director of the Department of Astrology in Beijing. Another Jesuit, Cristovão Ferreira, studied in Macao for ten years before setting off to spread the word in Japan. As head of the mission he was captured in 1633 and heavily persecuted, renouncing his faith under 'ditch torture' (he was hung up by his feet and buried to waist level in a hole dug in the ground). Some years later he wrote an anti-Christian pamphlet, *Deceit*

Unveiled, and put himself at the service of the Japanese Inquisition. His apostasy caused consternation in Macao and several emissaries were secretly dispatched to bring him back to God. They failed.

Until the expulsion of the Jesuits (which took effect in Macao in 1762), the Madre de Deus College remained the most important Christian centre of oriental studies. It was destroyed in 1835, in a fire that also ravaged the church next door, a monument of Christian art in Asia. But the Jesuit 'business of seduction' (Jacques Gernet) in China had come to a sudden end with the 'quarrel over rites', long before these symbols of the Christian presence on Chinese soil were destroyed. The debate over whether or not Chinese converts could still venerate their ancestors was kindled by the Dominicans in their rivalry with the Jesuits, causing agitation in Europe in the early 1700s. The Holy See gave a negative ruling in 1704, and two papal bulls in 1715 and 1742 prohibited the baptism of those Chinese who refused to renounce the worship of their ancestors. This decision aroused the wrath of the Jesuits in Macao, so much so that the papal legate, Mgr Maillard de Tournon, who was charged with notifying Beijing of the pontifical decision, was imprisoned. He was to die in Macao in 1710, of ill treatment, or worse.

China's attitude towards the missionaries had already begun to change. Initial trust gave way to suspicion. Rome's decision not only put an end to Valignano's politics of conciliation and adaptation, but provoked hostility as xenophobic reactions began to emerge. The exclusive nature of the Faith offended Chinese syncretism, and the Jesuits' manifest concern with adaptation together with the analogies they attempted to draw between Christian and Chinese values were perceived by certain scholars as duplicitous. So Macao became a refuge for missionaries fleeing intermittent persecution. A few years after the 1692 Edict of Tolerance, the missionaries were threatened with banishment if they failed to sign a declaration of allegiance to the ritual order of the

Empire. Most of them were obedient to Rome, and found themselves expelled for refusing.

And so, from the 1750s, the great plan for exchanging knowledge begun under the aegis of Alessandro Valignano and Matteo Ricci, came to an abrupt end. The undertaking had certainly been motivated by religious preoccupations (converting the leaders of the Empire more easily) and was tainted through identifying the Christian faith with Western science. But the presence of Jesuits in China was, according to Joseph Needham, historian of Chinese science and civilization, an authentic cross-cultural meeting for all that. And once this process was under way, Macao remained the link between two civilizations from the opposite ends of the world right up until the 19th century.

This exchange of knowledge started with geography and cartography, a field of deep and ongoing collaboration between the Jesuits and the Chinese. And it was through the enclave that China became acquainted with some of the wonders of Western technology: from clocks to the most complicated astronomical equipment, and *mappa mundi* to telescopes by way of automata (rabbits clanging cymbals, or birds in golden cages) and music-boxes, which were plundered by Anglo-French troops during the sacking of the Summer Palace in Beijing in 1860. Western painting techniques (perspective and *chiaroscuro*) were introduced to the court of the Chinese emperor by the Italian Jesuit Giuseppe Castiglione (1688–1766), an architect and gifted painter who arrived in Macao in 1715. It was he who exposed the Chinese to the kind of Baroque architecture that influenced the 'Chinese-ified' European style of the ornate pavilions at the Summer Palace. The gardens boasted lakes and fountains modelled on those at Versailles: these 'follies' had fallen to rack and ruin long before they were pillaged.

Conversely, it was through Macao (and again largely through the intervention of the Jesuits) that the West began to amass and organize its knowledge of China. It did so initially in the form of the first Sino-Portuguese dictionary (1584), which transcribed the ideograms phonetically and then, in more organized fashion, with the *Missione legatorum Iaponesium ad Romanam curiam* compiled by Fathers Duarte de Sande (Rector of São Paulo College) and Alessandro Valignano. Published in 1590, it was the first work printed in Macao to offer an introduction to the civilizations of China and Japan. In addition, the enclave became a centre for translation and training interpreters from Chinese and Japanese into Latin and Portuguese. They were concerned not only with religious and philosophical vocabularies, but with everyday language too. Words like *comprador* (referring to intermediaries working for foreign merchants), *mandarin* and *bamboo* (from the Luso-Malaysian dialect) were coined in Macao. Later, there were Macao-trained missionaries who transcribed Vietnamese into the Latin alphabet.

While China discovered American crops (cassava, yams, sweet potatoes, peanuts) via Macao, Europe for its part, and mostly thanks to the agency of the enclave, would taste a fine beverage: tea. Reaching Holland in the early 1600s, this 'herb from which the Chinese extract a delicate sap' (the name derives from *te* : the Amoy dialect in Fujian) shifted from a medical application to more popularized usage after Queen Catherine of Braganza introduced it to the English court. Charles II's Portuguese wife had encountered tea, called *chá* in her native language (from the Cantonese *chá*), through the Macao traders: the navigator Jorge Álvares, who arrived in Japan in 1547, was the first to mention the use of tea in the Japanese archipelago. Tea would become the object of frenzied trade (and trafficking) between Asia and Europe from the late 17th century.

It was through Macao, where the first hospital to offer Western medicine in Asia was opened in 1569, that the smallpox vaccination was introduced to China and, in return, that the Chinese pharmacopoeia and traditional medicines came to Europe (chiefly thanks to a French doctor practising in

60

Macao in the 18th century). It was also in Macao that liberal ideas began to have an impact on Chinese soil: the first Western-style newspaper in the Far East was published in the enclave in 1822: *Abelha da China* (*The Bee of China*), edited by a Dominican Father. Japan had of course produced information sheets called *kawaraban*, that were sold on street corners and reported all the city's major news, since the 1600s. But, short-lived as it was, *The Bee of China* also offered comment. And it was in Macao as well as Canton that the French amateur photographer Jules Itier took what are considered to be the first photographs of China, in 1844.

Through Macao, the world's intellectual horizons began to expand. For China, which thought of itself as the 'centre of the world', this meant the discovery of Western science; for Europe, which wanted to convey 'universal values', this meant an encounter of quite a different order. For the first time, Europeans were faced with civilizations comparable in many ways with their own. Travelling along the Silk Route, Chinese art had certainly influenced the Siennese school of the Trecento. But the early 17th century wasn't just about influence: Christian Europe was in the presence of one of the great religions of humanity: Buddhism. And it discovered different ways of being in the world as well as methods of thinking just as devel-oped as its own: it discovered nothing less than 'another humanity' (Jacques Gernet).

The Jesuits had in some way 'invented' this embellished, mythologized China (and in so doing set themselves up as necessary intermediaries between Beijing and the West, until the Dominicans crushed their morale in the quarrel over rites) which became a sort of mirror to 18th century Europe, magni-fied with its own myths, a prop to its positive and negative utopias – a phenomenon that continued until the end of the 20th century and spread to Japan.) The Middle Kingdom provided the philosophers of the Enlightenment with a pretext for criticizing the abuses of religion and the *Ancien Régime*. The Luminaries held up mandarin values as an example of the civil order they'd been seeking to develop: an order based on merit not privilege. Confucius was transformed into a model of atheist virtue, the 'Socrates of Asia'. But following the American Revolution and the rise of bourgeois Europe, a fascination with the Middle Kingdom gave way to condescension and the urge to 'enlighten' China (and, beyond it, the rest of the region), whose exception to the rule was perceived as a breach of 'natural rights' – before intervening by force to secure trade interests. From then on, contact with Asia was played out at an invasive and exploitative level: cannon fire succeeded the litany of sermons. But that's another story.

This contact between two ways of being in the world, of which Macao was the intermediary, gave rise to much distrust and misunderstanding. The opposite ends of the world had brushed up against each other and caught a glimpse of something, but in the final count they had kept their distance, remaining strangers to one another. And yet the tentative spiritual *rapprochement* initiated by the Jesuits was perhaps without parallel in the history of humanity. The microcosm of Macao was one of the fruits of this encounter: a strange 'Baroque theatre of the world', in the words of Arthur Chen.

At the height of its prosperity (1550–1650), the enclave was a city of wealth and splendour unparalleled in the Portuguese empire.

A city of adventurers basking in their wealth but aware they might have to fight to defend it at any time. Bold and superstitious, hospitable and remarkably tolerant towards the foreigner who came in peace; they went about their business and practised their religions in churches with golden-skinned women from Malacca and African slaves.

Austin Coates's rather idealized vision still contains a grain of truth. The enclave's splendour was reflected in the architecture of the houses along the Praia Grande, in that of

Santa Casa de Misericórdia.

the churches and in a colonial art steeped in European and Asian influences.

The churches are the greatest testimony to Macao's glorious past. Travellers visiting the enclave towards the end of the 19th century were struck by how many there were for such a small city (ten, to be precise). Even today, whether you're a Christian or not, you can't help becoming a pilgrim in this city where the stone saints hold their crosses up to an Asian sky.

Churches and religious establishments were among the first buildings in Macao. While the Jesuits were erecting the college and church of Madre de Deus (São Paulo), the Spanish Dominicans were building a monastery and São Domingos church at the tip of an isosceles triangle formed by the city's central plaza and closed off at its base by the Senado. Boasting an elegant façade of stucco moulding, and pierced by wide windows and heavy doors, São Domingos was closely linked to life in Macao because of its central position near to a market. It was on the plaza in front of the church that antagonism between Dominicans and Jesuits gave rise to a few nasty skirmishes between the Brothers and the authorities in 1707. On the right of the plaza stands the Santa Casa de Misericórdia, a small neo-classical building (rebuilt in the 19th century, as was the Senado). The city's oldest relics are to be found in this Holy House: a full-length portrait of its founder, the Jesuit Dom Melchior Craneiro, who was a contemporary of Francisco Xavier and the first Bishop of Macao. He also built the paupers' hospital (Hospital dos Pobres, which later became the São Rafael Hospital), where, from the 1590s, Western medicine was practised for the first time in Asia. Dom Melchior laid the foundations of political organization both in the city and the Senado. The prelate's cranium is displayed in a reliquary on a table in the Casa's reception room, between an hour-glass and a small bell.

São Domingos and the São José Seminary contain paintings and figurines in ivory and wood exemplifying the local art that, minor though it may have been, was unique to Macao in its treatment of European and Christian motifs by Asian artists. Such eclecticism is also to be found in the layout of gardens.

A city of God, a city of trade, and a fortified city, Macao was also a city of the arts. There are few remaining examples of Macao's secular art. But César Guillen-Nuñez suggests that its religious paintings (a pietà, for example, whose Virgin and Christ have oriental eyes, kept in the São José Seminary) and the São Lourenço crucifix made from wood, gold and ivory, point to the existence of a 'Macao school'. It would have been founded by an Italian Jesuit from Naples, Giovanni Niccolo, who fled the persecutions in Japan and was responsible for the interior decoration of São Paulo Church.

In India and Japan, where places of worship were cluttered

São Paulo church, before 1874.

with pious representations, Xavier became convinced of the importance of the image as an aid to preaching. Not enough paintings and engravings were brought over from Europe. In addition, as soon as Alessandro Valignano arrived in Japan, he decided to open an Academy of Fine Arts in 1583 under the direction of Giovanni Niccolo. An artist with many talents, Niccolo taught there until he was forced to seek refuge in Macao (in 1614). There flowed from this academy a series of oil paintings, watercolours and engravings in which the art of the Counter-Reformation, introduced into Asia via the missions, later mingled with local influences. Few examples of Christian art survived in Japan at the time of the persecutions; more can be found in Macao.

The church of São Paulo, of which only the façade remains, was without doubt the jewel of the enclave: a masterpiece in its own right and the pinnacle of Christian art in the Far East. Like Saint Mark's in Venice, a meeting point of Byzantine and Roman art, São Paulo was a fusion of Western and Asian influences. It astonished travellers: 'The church is among the most magnificent I've seen, even in Italy, with the exception of Saint Peter's', wrote the French Jesuit Alexandre de Rhodes at the beginning of the 17th century. At the same time, the Englishman Peter Mundy evokes for his part the 'spacious interior architecture with three stone arches', a 'marvellous' curved and decorated ceiling, and 'the brilliance of walls covered from ceiling to floor in gold, and wooden sculptures painted in exquisite colours.'

The church was designed by the Italian Jesuit Carlo Spinola (martyred in Japan), who drew inspiration from the Baroque splendour of the Gésu Church in Rome. But São Paulo, on which construction began in 1602 reaching completion in 1640, was above all the work of Chinese and Japanese artists and artisans working under the orders of the Jesuit Fathers and applying techniques such as *chiaroscuro*, unknown in this part of the world. The church was embellished with a magnificent clock, a gift from Louis XIV as a token of his gratitude for the help Macao had given the French Jesuits; it rang time for the whole city. César Guillen-Nuñez believes this cosmopolitan masterpiece to be a work of art epitomizing the 'climate of tolerance' which characterized Macao.

Built entirely of wood, the church and college next door were destroyed in a fire in 1835, leaving only the vast granite façade decorated with ten columns which still stand. Following the dissolution of the Society of Jesus, a garrison of soldiers had taken up quarters at the school. The fire began in the kitchen. Among the motifs of the majestic 'stone sermon' as the façade is known, is a Madonna holding the head not of a snake, the symbol of evil, but of a seven-headed dragon, the Asian embodiment of power, which she appears to govern more than overwhelm. To the side, a galleon is depicted in full sail. Statues of saints (Ignatius Loyola, Francisco Xavier) adorn the alcoves. One of them shelters a stone skeleton pierced through with arrows bearing the ideogrammatic inscription: 'He who remembers death, will never be a sinner.'

São Paulo's façade offers a distillation of the message brought by the Jesuits to Asia. But its iconographic features, taken from local culture, are also symptomatic of the proselytizing drive to adapt this message. Today, with its entrances gaping to the sky like unseeing eyes, São Paulo's façade is a metaphor for the destiny of human ambitions: Christian hope carved in stone disappears into the emptiness of the Asian sky. In the evenings, when you climb that great deserted stairway leading up to it, the grey stone stands out against the silken night like a wrinkled face whose features are hard to distinguish: a mask whose features have disappeared into the vast realm of shadow.

Two centuries before the fire transformed this symbol of Macao's golden age into a relic, the wind had already changed for the enclave. The delicate balance of its prosperity was overturned within the space of a few years, during the first half of the 17th century. First and foremost, English and Dutch competitors turned up in the region, damaging the Portuguese trade monopoly. The latter actually attacked Macao in 1622, but were driven back into the sea by a motley army of priests, African slaves and merchants. More seriously, Japan, the pole of lucrative trade in the Goa–Macao–Nagasaki route, closed itself to foreigners. The Portuguese were driven out (1638) and only the Dutch were authorized to stay, confined to the minuscule islet of Dejima by Nagasaki. Blamed for the arrival of four English ships that had sailed up the Pearl river without Chinese permission, and whose crews indulged in extortion, the Portuguese also saw themselves cut off from Canton. Then came a fresh piece of bad luck: Portugal broke off its alliance with Spain, so Macao lost the route to Manila and consequently to South America. In 1641 the Dutch seized possession of Malacca, breaking the route on which Macao's prosperity had been built in yet another place. The Portuguese were losing their land bases as well as control of the seas.

In the space of a dozen years, a cataclysm rained down on Macao. The impoverished enclave – for whom the trade in sandalwood from Timor was one of its last remaining assets – enlisted in endless Portuguese-led battles to put down uprisings on the island. The new maritime routes were mostly restricted to the China Sea and would never be as lucrative as the 'Japanese route', although the 'Cochin-China route' brought about an increase in activity at the end of the 18th century. Travellers staying in Macao early in the following century described it as a beautiful city, but languishing to the point of ruin. And yet this decline would help shape Macao's identity. The enclave had discovered isolation, and its inhabitants began to forge a unique culture for themselves, albeit one still influenced by Portugal and China.

The trade setbacks that brought about Macao's ruin were overtaken by another crisis: that of the Middle Kingdom. When civil war broke out in 1644 after the Manchurian conquest of the south, there was an influx of refugees. These immigrants swelled the enclave's population, which temporarily reached 40,000.

Macao began to change in a long and slow process of, to use the expression coined by Louis Dermigny, 'absorption by women and its environment'.

A Mecanese-style pavilion.

Incense, Compradors, Opium and Slaves

The charming white ceramic plaques with pale blue lettering
and borders announcing the street names in Macao are a good
example of the enclave's ambiguous status. You'll find two
topographies superimposed. The Portuguese names consecrate
a hero, a saint or a locality. But the ideograms that run from top
to bottom on the right-hand side of the plaque often refer to
something else. Sometimes the Portuguese actually preferred a
street's Chinese name to its Christian one. The principal artery
that splices the city on a south-east/north-west axis, from the
Praia Grande to the Inner Harbour passing in front of the
Senado is, for example, called the Avenida da Almeida Ribeiro.
Named after a Colonial Secretary who never set foot in Macao,
but who none the less authorized the construction of a thor-
oughfare that carved up the tangle of streets in the Chinese
quarter in the early 1900s, the Avenida ran the risk of cutting off
the tail belonging to the dragon supposed to sleep there. The
Chinese didn't know who Almeida Ribeiro was, and, more
appealingly, called the new road San Ma Lou: the Street of
Horses. It was also a more realistic name, since the thorough-
fare was one of the city's rare arteries wide enough for two
horses harnessed abreast. Plenty of Portuguese now refer to it
by its Chinese name.

Sometimes the Chinese and Portuguese names coincide.
Take the Rua da Felicidade, for example. A typically narrow
street flanked by low houses in the Chinese town, it runs down
towards the Inner Harbour. From the 1850s to the early 1900s,
it was a meeting place for intellectual bohemians; well known
for its pleasure houses, it inspired journalists and writers in
search of China's 'mysteries'. The Chinese kept its Portuguese

name, simply adding a superlative to make it the 'Street of Great Happiness'. It is rare, however, for a street to be named after an illustrious Chinese figure, or a Buddhist monk, and rarer still for one to celebrate a non-Catholic religious dignitary. Lou Lim Iok, a Chinese aristocrat and patron of the arts with republican ideas, who escaped to Macao in the early 20th century to avoid being the target of a nationalist offensive, has secured a place in the history books thanks to the beautiful garden named in his honour and modelled on the famous gardens of Suzhou in China.

There are two parallel universes reflected in these street signs. Two worlds that have co-existed and rubbed shoulders because that was the way history and residential interests wanted it, but without really merging or becoming promiscuous. There are certainly two cities in Macao, a Christian one and a Chinese one. But there is also a third: the Creole city.

Once the golden age of triangular trade in the 1650s was over, Macao owed its survival and relative prosperity more to its Chinese and Macanese (mixed-race) traders than to the Portuguese. From a city of pioneers, merchant adventurers, missionaries and soldiers, a transitory population with one eye on the ocean and beyond, Macao evolved into a city of permanent residents: 'A Eurasian and cosmopolitan city', as Jonathan Porter has written. The first Portuguese claimed to be representatives of their birth country, where they hoped to return one day. They formed a community of men whose wives and concubines came mostly from Malacca and India. But it was a long time before the Chinese lived in the city. With the exception of seminarians and interpreters, they came to work as domestics or to sell their products, before setting off again in the evening towards the village of Wangxia 'outside the walls'. They weren't authorized to emigrate to Macao until 1793, when artisans, hawkers, shopkeepers and *compradores* (intermediaries) from Guandong and Fujian flocked to settle there. Troubles on the mainland (the White Lotus and Taiping rebellions triggered social instability in the Canton region) intensified this immigration. The new arrivals clustered around the Inner Harbour, along the Praia Manduco and at the foot of Penha Hill. The bay was subsequently filled in and lost its natural curve, but the streets of the old 'bazaar' district stick to their original course, hugging a shoreline that no longer exists. At the same time, Macao became more integrated into the economic life of the hinterland. The growth in the Chinese population also gave rise to a new form of criminal activity of which one notable victim was the Governor João Maria Ferreira do Amaral, assassinated in 1849. This was the first spectacular demonstration of the presence of triads (secret societies) in Macao.

Above all, the new arrivals brought their beliefs and shrines with them, and Macao became even more steeped in Chinese customs. Temples were originally built outside the city. This was true of the temple dedicated to A-Ma, protector of fishermen, situated at the foot of Barra Hill, which existed in a more primitive form before the Portuguese arrived. Its pavilions seem to climb to the pinnacle of a hill lost in the foliage of ancient Indian fig trees. The temple has been restored time and again but, as is often the case in Macao, the images bequeathed by Chinnery and Borget remain etched on the memory. If we're to believe Mgr Teixiera, the cult of A-Ma, the avatar of Guan Yin the compassionate, was readily accepted by the Portuguese because of a tendency to confuse it with the cult of Mary, also protector of sailors: like A-Ma, to whom the small shrines on Chinese junks are dedicated, Mary is present in one form or another on board Portuguese boats. The most important temple in Macao is consecrated to Guan Yin. A great figure of compassion, this divinity is honoured in temples throughout the enclave, but the Guan Yin Tang, located to the north of the peninsula in what used to be Wangxia village, is the most impressive. This Buddhist temple predates the arrival of the Portuguese and was, for a long time, the seat of the magistrate charged with administering the affairs of the Chinese population as well as being the residence for officials posted to Macao. It was on a stone table in its garden that the

Treaty of Wangxia was signed between the United States and China in 1844, after the conclusion of the first Opium War between the Chinese and British.

As the Chinese town developed, temples and shrines sprang up everywhere; and the oldest were rebuilt. Even today, Macao is a city that smells of incense. Its fragrance hangs in the air around the great temples and unexpectedly follows strollers, emanating from countless tiny crude shrines dedicated to a local divinity, the sticks of incense burning in front of them replaced by neighbours. With its profusion of forms of worship, Macao is one of the rare places in China today where ancestral traditions and popular beliefs have been preserved.

When the Chinese immigrants arrived, the urban culture ceased to be predominantly European. Large houses with huge verandahs and pot-bellied balconies in the east of the city are matched by compact homes in the west, taller than they are wide and crammed together with their small windows in the Southern Chinese style. Their iron gates have ornamental apertures at the top or are made of wire mesh to let the air through. Chinese immigration also led to the emergence of ground floor shops, with the owner and his family living above. And so the colourful 'bazaar' district was born, its

> narrow streets lined with shops and a busy crowd continu-
> ally passing through. Here, a porter with a pole on his
> shoulder and a bundle swaying from either end; there, a
> young boat-woman passing quickly by, her head hooded by
> a silk handkerchief, with her long blue cotton jacket and
> wide trousers and her pretty bare feet spared from fashion-
> able mutilation . . .

as wrote Théophile de Ferrière Le Vayer in the 1850s. 'Barbers, cooks and greengrocers spread their wares on street corners and at crossroads, heedless of the wind'. Once again the images of the past tend to be superimposed on the present.

The A-Ma temple at Macao, then and now.

Following the trade crisis and the rise of the Dutch influence on the seas at the end of the 18th century, the number of inhabitants of pure Portuguese stock dwindled, but there was a growing population of Eurasians known as *casados*. They formed a new class of resident merchants and forged a unique 'Creole' culture. They also afforded the city an unusual status by resisting the authority of Goa, capital of the Lusitanian Empire in their part of the world. When Portugal temporarily came under the Spanish yoke from 1580 to 1640, the Senado of Macao, then enjoying its golden age, remained faithful to the Portuguese crown; once Portugal recovered its sovereignty, the honorific title of Leal Senado (the 'loyal senate') was conferred on it. These 'sons of the land' (*filhos da terra*) were born from marriages or relationships between Portuguese, Indians, Malays, Japanese (Christians sheltered in Macao at the time of the persecutions) and Chinese. Rarely has a microcosm been so cosmopolitan, or brought together so many different races and cultures. In addition to Europeans, East Indians and Eurasians there were people from Timor and African slaves brought over from Angola and Mozambique. La Pérouse, who visited Macao in 1787, estimated that out of the 20,000 inhabitants in the enclave at the time, scarcely more than a hundred were Portuguese by birth, whereas there were 2,000 *mestizos* (the rest of the population was Asian and primarily Chinese).

The mixing of bodies in Macao is expressed in a hybrid of cultures, notably in the city's architecture. From the late 17th century, the neo-Classical style gave way to less pretentious architecture combining the joint influences of European and Chinese aesthetics in a form altogether better suited to life in the tropics. Developed during the 18th and 19th centuries, this exclusively Macanese architecture was replaced by a more international and anonymous style at the beginning of the 20th century.

Purists comment on the 'clumsiness' of the European-style architecture in Macao. But imperfections and unintentional

The Praia Grande.

pastiches were one of the city's outmoded architectural charms. Macanese artisans and artists have, for a long time, built and decorated edifices as if they were souvenirs, intended as mementos or versions of previous models. The architect Carlos Marreiros observes how they've also integrated local elements and personal flourishes into their creations.

The architecture of Macanese houses combines the layout of Chinese dwellings (designed around an inner courtyard) with borrowings from the Southern European style: ornamental motifs, wrought-iron balconies and verandahs with large French windows to let in the fresh morning air or keep the rooms cool in the afternoon when the shutters are closed. Mediterranean from the outside, many houses were of Chinese design inside. This was especially the case for most of the houses along the Praia Grande. Macanese architecture also incorporates local traditions: notably geomancy (the siting and

The Praia Grande after the 1874 typhoon.

orientation of buildings in accordance with natural forms). In addition, it became customary to paint the outsides of houses in pastel colours: yellow, green, pink and blue. But they were affected by the humidity and soon looked faded and washed out, their patina of infinitely varied shades accentuating the city's drowsy decadence: the elegantly relaxed environment reflected its economic lethargy.

In a satirical sonnet, the poet Barbosa du Bocage, who stayed in Macao at the very end of the 18th century, offered this description:

> *A governor without authority, a bishop just the same,*
> *A hideout for virtuous nuns*
> *Three monasteries, five thousand*
> *Nhons . . . and a wretched workforce of Chinese Christians*

Much poverty, plenty of vile women
And a hundred Portuguese, all in one enclave . . .
This is what Portugal possesses in Macao.

Acerbic it may be, but his observation is not without truth. Twice during the 19th entury, Macao hoped to regain its position as a trading centre: first through the traffic in opium and then in coolies. The enclave had temporarily benefited from the tough line against foreigners taken by the Chinese in the early 18th century: this disrupted the lucrative trade in tea, which had been all the rage among the European elite since the previous century, having superseded silk as China's principal export. Macao's merchants – most of them Eurasian – could trade more freely in Canton, while Westerners who only had contact with Chinese merchant guilds were faced with a sort of collegiate trade monopoly. But it was a flash in the pan. Macao's trading role with China continued to deteriorate: the deathblow was struck when China's ports opened to foreigners and Hong Kong was taken by the British following the Opium Wars (1839–43 and 1856–60).

The enforced opening of five major Chinese ports and the loss of trade monopoly by the East India Company (1833) gave elbow room to 'private' merchants involved in smuggling what the Chinese, with haughty disdain, referred to as 'foreign filth' (opium). The East India Company initiated this trafficking, not directly (because it represented the British Crown), but through the agency of buccaneers. The major trade at the time was in tea, with Britain and Continental Europe developing a real taste for it. But the irksome Chinese bureaucracy made for tough trading: 'Not a cup of tea is drunk in Europe that hasn't caused humiliation to those who bought it in Canton', wrote La Pérouse, in the late 18th century. In return, the Company sold Indian cotton to China, but the revenue far from compensated the costs of importing tea. There was only one product the Chinese consumed in sufficient quantities, and that was opium. The Company had vast poppy fields in Bengal at its disposal. But it soon realized the drug was ruining its 'human resources' when it was sold on the Indian market, and in the long term this risked incurring more loss than gain. These considerations, together with the need to find a 'currency of exchange' in order to offset the costs of purchasing tea, made the East India Company decide to attack the Chinese market with opium. Given that the Son of Heaven had banned the drug being introduced, recourse to contraband was the only option. The traffic developed quickly with the help of corruption, and it proved highly lucrative: there was an increase from 2,000 bundles of opium in 1793 to 26,000 by 1830. In the five years that followed the opening of the ports after the Treaty of Nankin (1842), the volume doubled (52,000 bundles) attracting new traffickers of every nationality to the region.

Foreigners didn't have the right to settle permanently in Canton until China was opened up by force, so the new European arrivals based themselves in Macao, which became a holiday resort between spells of business dealings: up in its hills, they coped better with the heat and typhoons. A case in point was William Jardine, a British doctor with the Merchant Navy who had sniffed out opium in India and quickly transformed himself into a smuggler. The Chinese nicknamed him 'Old Rat with Iron Head' after he took a bludgeoning on the skull without turning a hair. George Chinnery painted a portrait of this opium prince in 1832. Seated at a table holding a dip pen in his right hand, his relatively coarse features, fleshy lips, disproportionately long eagle's beak of a nose and disdainful pout make him a rather unsympathetic subject. The ruthless merchant was then at the height of his powers and already only had one idea in mind: to convince London to send a task force to China in order to procure the right freely to stupefy an entire nation. There was another opium 'prince' living on the 'hill' of Macao at the time, an American called Herbert Dent who lived in the delightful pink palace, Santa Sancha, which later became the Residence of the Portuguese

Governor of Macao until the time of the handover.

Opium trafficking in Macao had its lascars as well as its princes, some of them rather surprising. When Protestant missionaries settled in the enclave at the beginning of the 19th century, their presence was viewed rather acrimoniously by the Catholic Fathers and Brothers of the plaza. One of these 'holy men' wasn't quite white as snow: in the name of spreading the faith, the Revd Charles Gutzlaff agreed to serve the interests of William Jardine. This Prussian missionary doctor, 'short of leg and wide of face', distributed bibles and edifying tracts in the coastal villages where his English wife also taught. Jardine was primarily interested in the Revd's linguistic abilities: he spoke Cantonese and the local dialects fluently. After 'lengthy deliberation', Charles Gutzlaff agreed to embark on one of Jardine's ships, the *Sylph*, where he would act as the smugglers' interpreter while preaching the gospel all the way to North China. Souls were to be exchanged for a few bundles of opium that would intoxicate other, or sometimes the same, souls. Their salvation lay in the hands of Providence.

By the beginning of the 19th century, it rapidly became clear that the merchants of Macao were no match for their powerful British counterparts, who were supported by the Crown and the London banking community. The Portuguese enclave could only play a part in the new trade networks if it remained subordinate to and within the sphere of British interests. The lucrative trafficking in opium was a case in point. Macao hadn't always just been a holiday resort where foreigners liked to stay. According to Louis Dermigny, 'this scrap of a vanished empire had become an annexe or, better, a necessary antechamber for the English' in Sino-Indian trade, and in particular the smuggling of opium. So useful was it, that the British openly tried to appropriate the territory on two occasions (1802 and 1808). They failed, but managed to supplant Macao's merchants when it came to opium trafficking, much to the detriment of the latter who had harboured hopes of profits and even a renaissance of their past glory.

The Inner Harbour in the 1950s.

Macao became the centre of opium smuggling in the early 19th century, based on Lusitanian–British collaboration. The enclave had already been selling opium to the Chinese for decades, brought from the Portuguese possessions in Malwa, north of Bombay. But trade never took off in the way it did under the British. Omnipresent in the region, the British attracted Armenians and Indian Parsees in their wake. Following the Son of Heaven's august prohibition of 1799 outlawing opium, smuggling simply shifted from the Pearl river towards the enclave. Traffic prospered handsomely from 1800 to 1815: 'You can see opium being openly transported in broad daylight through the streets', wrote a Russian traveller staying in Macao at the time. The drug was then sent as far as Canton in a convoy of 'opium boats', or 'long streamlined junks piloted by armed men'. The Macanese wanted to outwit the British by overtaking the network of opium from Bengal with opium from Malwa, bought at their own expense in Goa. This proved the cause of rupture: the British transferred their traffic onto huge boats which lay, armed like forts, at anchor in the Pearl river. They were driven off by the Chinese but, contrary to the expectations of the Macanese who thought they had brought them to bay, they never returned to the enclave, moving instead to the island of Lintin, where no one was likely to bother them.

And so Macao was evicted from wholesale opium trafficking. In addition, when Beijing decided to react against the massive influx of 'foreign filth', Macao adopted a neutral position so as to avoid having China blockade its imports of provisions and other supplies. In the course of the First Opium War, the European presence in Macao increased again with the arrival of refugees. Adrião Acácio da Silveira Pinto, the Governor at the time, was under pressure from the Chinese who were threatening to invade Macao, and eventually warned the British that he could no longer guarantee their safety if they didn't get out: the entire community boarded boats that reassembled in Hong Kong harbour. Meanwhile, there was growing unrest in London. Palmerston ended up giving way to William Jardine's persistent lobbying. The First Opium War had begun.

The British were determined to carve themselves a foothold on Chinese soil where they could carry out their business without having to rely on Portuguese goodwill. Following their victory over China, they appropriated Hong Kong: Beijing ceded the island to Great Britain in perpetuity under the Treaty of Nanking. Portugal took advantage of China's defeat to demand that Macao be granted autonomous status: in 1845, the enclave became a free port. Forty years later, the territory was conceded to Lisbon for perpetuity. Meanwhile, the deep-water port of Hong Kong had largely superseded the enclave in the China trade. The opening up of certain ports to foreigners had, in any case, reduced interest in Macao as a trading base. But ironically, Chinese intermediaries used by foreign merchants in

A wharf at the Inner Harbour, 1950s.

Canton have gone down in history under the name given to them by the Portuguese, who were the first to institutionalize the system: *compradores*. These intermediaries were attached to a foreign company and recognized by the Chinese authorities, their responsibilities consisting initially of overseeing the loading and unloading of boats in Canton on behalf of Macao merchants. Later, their functions extended to purchasing, recruiting local personnel, accounting and managing all transactions with the Chinese authorities.

Macao had 'failed' as far as opium trafficking was concerned. But you could say it recovered lost ground through its trafficking in coolies, supplying the plantations, mines and colonial enterprises of Australia, Cuba and Peru, and also the British West Indies and the Philippines with a ruthlessly exploited workforce.

The Chinese port of Amoy was the original centre for trafficking in coolies (the first 'cargo' of coolies set out from there in 1845 on French ships bound for the Île de Bourbon, now known as Reunion). But an uprising a few years later forced the coolie merchants to find somewhere else for their trafficking. The ambiguous status of the Portuguese enclave, together with legislation more relaxed than Hong Kong's (Great Britain was a signatory to the Treaty of Ghent of 1814, prohibiting the trade in African slaves) and its old links with the ports of South-East Asia made Macao an ideal choice. Add to that a shady bunch of racketeers who were already active in the sale of coolies, controlling the local traffic in drugs and prostitution as well as exerting a ruthless hold over the enclave, and Macao had all the necessary 'qualifications'. Lisbon tacitly encouraged the trafficking without any great 'scruples'.

A large number of Macao merchants were involved in a trade that, in its scale and inhumanity, rivalled the middle passage of African slaves across the Atlantic. Five 'agencies' with 130 employees were operating out of Macao in 1870. Trafficking prospered for nearly twenty years, between 1856 and 1874. The coolies were often recruited in the delta region and herded together into *barracões* (camps), which were essentially prisons, where they were kept until the time came for them to leave, and were beaten if they didn't sign a 'voluntary' work indenture.

The Comte de Beauvoir made a stop-off in Macao in 1867, and describes at length in his *Journey Around the World*, published in 1875, what seemed to him 'the most characteristic aspect of Macao': the 'camps' or 'famous depots of the so-called "coolie emigration", more accurately branded the Chinese slave trade'. At the entrance to the 'shop' trading in human lives, the Comte de Beauvoir noticed paintings depicting 'luxurious ships' involved in coolie trafficking, and remarked that 'the French flag features far too often in these sad advertisements'.

I can see long corridors with 'Chinese destined for emigration' crammed into hangars on either side. There they are, waiting to leave, their faces distorted and their bodies pallid; scarcely clad by their rotten rags, they bear the most hideous stamp of foul poverty and lie in the most abominable squalor. The trade in Chinese slaves is a wholly deplorable story: although only nineteen years old, it includes the most horrible massacres, the most infamous speculations, and a thousand times more atrocities than the trade in African slaves which it replaced . . . Thousands of poor devils are seized by force or ensnared by deceit, before being shipped off to far-flung destinations without any form of regulation whatsoever.

Chained up or locked inside bamboo cages, many of the poor wretches perished in the course of a voyage that lasted more than 100 days. 'Five times out of ten there's a mutiny on board', continues the Comte de Beauvoir, 'and the European crew is mercilessly massacred, or else whole human cargoes die of suffocation in the hold because of the cruelty of an enraged captain.' The mortality rate reached 14 per cent. The coolies had to sign a contract, an example of which is offered by our author: 'I undertake to work twelve hours per day for eight years in the service of the owner of this contract and to renounce all freedom during that time. My master undertakes to feed me and give me four piastres a month, to clothe me and to free me the day this contract expires.'

Of the 322,000 coolies shipped abroad as 'beasts of burden' between 1845 and 1873, nearly half would have passed through Macao. They included women and girls who were often literally carried off: as was the case in Ning-Po for example, where the Portuguese Consul was in receipt of substantial 'dividends' in exchange for turning a blind eye. It wasn't until 1873 that Lisbon put a stop to the trafficking in coolies, thereby dealing a heavy blow to Macao's economy. And so ended one of the least glorious periods in the city's history.

Macao never regained its previous importance as a commercial centre, but the city had expanded. By the late 1800s its population amounted to 30,000 Chinese together with 5,000

Europeans and people of mixed race. Keen not to be left behind while other European countries were carving their empires in Asia, Macao decked itself out with administrative buildings (the Senado, the Clube Militar) in the neo-classical style. A private house on the Praia Grande became the seat of the Governor. Even so, the contradictions inherent in Macao's hybrid status became increasingly obvious. A European enclave in the China Sea, it was ostracized by its neighbours Vietnam and China for being in the camp of the Western powers threatening them and, despite being an Asian city that was part of the regional trading network, it was driven to the brink of ruin. It was symptomatic of Macao's contradictions at the time that the differences between the two cities, one Chinese the other Christian, became more pronounced. 'It's not that Macao has lost its ability to adapt to its Asian environ- ment. It's the environment that has transformed itself so radically there's no longer any room for trading communities like Macao and many other ports on the China Sea', explains Pierre-Yves Mangin.

Macao had begun its descent into serene inertia. A retired city, a pleasant abode for Europeans and rich Chinese, a city of languors and pleasures, of tolerance and turpitude: the gentle version of Macao we see painted by George Chinnery and again, at the beginning of the 20th century, in the photographs of John Thomson or, between the two World Wars, in the watercolours of the Russian immigrant George Smirnoff.

Macao changed very little until the 1960s. Markedly down at heel, it still kept up those appearances that seduced most 19th- century travellers in the days when the city was home to substantial merchants and traffickers of every nationality. On the 'hill' above the Praia Grande and along the riverbank winding in a harmonious curve at its base (likened rather exag- geratedly to the Bay of Naples, by the American Osmond Tiffany) stood the finest houses. Bourgainville wrote, in 1825, that 'the dazzling whiteness of its buildings' could be seen from afar. 'The [city] looks out to the east and the elegantly built, well-aligned houses along the water-front follow the shore's contours. The city's most beautiful quarter is the place where the foreigners live.' Théophile Ferrière Le Vayer's description, some twenty years later, is even more enthusiastic:

> We could soon make out the city with its forts and monasteries and churches; there, in a semi-circle by the shore, was a garland of houses in shades of white, pink, blue and yellow, seemingly the most delightful in the world; this was the famous Praia Grande esplanade, with the city rising up behind it in the form of an ampitheatre, verandah upon verandah, church upon church, garden upon garden.

The Comte de Beauvoir, on the other hand, was more acerbic: 'A chaos of houses painted in blue, green and red, with Southern European terraces for roof-tops, a dozen cathedral belfries, windows barricaded with iron bars, paved alleys two metres wide threading through sugar-loaf districts . . . welcome to Macao!' Beauvoir was even less flattering when it came to the inhabitants:

> What a strange people are the conquerors of this land! The descendants of Albuquerque who scurry along in crowds, hanging onto their sabres or wrapped in their scarves, form a race of Portuguese crossed with Chinese, the latter having already been crossed with a mixture of Malays, Indians and Negroes; in sum, a puny scrawny race, with pale chocolate skin, almond-shaped slit-eyes, vegetating in a climate that's part Christian and part pagan, part civilized and part Asian . . .

What fly was it that stung the Comte de Beauvoir, whose comments about Japan were, by contrast, so subtle? He didn't like the city, of that we can be sure. But, more seriously, he was unfair to it. Macao was a composite world where the worst rubbed shoulders with the best, but its saving grace was being hospitable and open to everyone: from die-hard adventurers to exiles, from refugees fleeing oppression to debtors escaping their creditors. Therein lies its greatness.

In Camões' garden, the memorial to the poet, set up in 1811.

A Land of Asylum, Exile and Adoption

The city is streaming with water. It's the rainy season. A sticky, salty humidity oozes its way along the walls, attacking and corroding everything: paint, stones, metal. Water combines with heat to feed the spongy mosses that abound, as well as the crazy clumps of grasses and the shrubs poking here and there between the roof tiles, clinging to the smallest crack. Green moss becomes embedded in column mouldings; rust gnaws at wrought-iron balconies. Macao in the rainy season is a city that smells of the earth, of humus. Large persistent raindrops drum down and bounce back off the balcony, forming a curtain that dissolves all contours. Taïpa has vanished, the grey and beige monochrome where sandy sea and leaden sky dissolve into one another is penetrated only by the glare of street lights from the motorway now blocking the Praia Grande: these beacons of doom are switched on even though it's daytime. Rain, and more rain. When Macao's like this there's no cure for melancholy, for that feeling of loss when you wake at dawn soaked in sweat and the silence is broken only by the beating of wind on shutters or the regular 'woosh-woosh' of the fan on the ceiling. The storm brings a hint of cool. And suddenly, you feel almost chilled to the bone. As blurred silhouettes lashed by flurries of rain hurry along by the walls of deserted streets, this Macao streaming with warm water gives off not so much an impression of termination and death as of exhaustion and pathetic solitude.

Weighed down with water, the net curtains seem weary of the damp and gentle wind stirring them, and they flap unconvincingly. Their movement unexpectedly brings to mind the white linen robes worn by the poet who used to live a few hundred metres down hill, in a dark house giving onto the

Praia Grande. Camílio Pessanha was one of Macao's celebrated figures at the turn of the 19th century: a macabre character whose soul was in exile. At least he wasn't booed on arrival in the enclave, as was Oscar Wilde who fled to Naples at roughly the same time to escape public denunciation of his practices. Like Wilde, however, this young and brilliant barrister was rebellious and non-conformist in his thinking. More a poet than a lawyer, and bruised by a secret love, he had led a Bohemian life in Coimbra, becoming a dedicated absinthe drinker. When the Portuguese Governor was looking for candidates to teach in Macao, Pessanha jumped at the chance. And so began a perpetual exile. He arrived in Macao in 1894 and died there in 1926. He practised as a teacher, a barrister and a temporary court registrar. In Macao, Pessanha exchanged the grog-shop of absinthe for the hallucinatory stupor of opium. Lost in exile, he wrote poems in the style of Mallarmé, and spent the final phase of his 'pilgrimage through life' cloistered in his treasure-trove of a house that gave onto the Praia Grande, like 'a Pharaoh in his tomb'. His black beard, deep-set eyes, hollow face and emaciated body are said to have made him look like a fakir. Clad only in linen robes, stretched out on a huge square bed buried in books, his opium pipe to hand, he conversed with his visitors on the subjects of poetry and Chinese art. From one mirage to another, 'lost in a lost country', the poet seemed to accept mankind's destiny with calm and ironic detachment, 'without coveting or regretting what was lost or never happened'. In a letter to a friend, Carlos Amaro, he did, however, express the desire 'never to arrive where I'm going, but to travel forever on a ship bound for nowhere'.

Throughout its history Macao has been at the far end of the world, a land of exile but also of shelter and adoption. It has had its share of famous exiles. The first would have been Luis Vaz de Camões (1524–80), Portugal's national poet, said to have written sections of his epic *The Lusiads* there. But there's no trace of his stay, which is still the subject of conjecture today. Camões was banished by the King of Portugal, and it was perhaps during his voyage to Goa and the Molucca Islands between 1556 and 1558 that he stayed in Macao, shortly after the arrival of the first merchant traders. A cave, formed by three rocks that used to overlook the Inner Harbour, has been celebrated since the 1600s as the place where the one-eyed poet allegedly wrote some cantos of his epic poem. Portugal's determination to link Camões to the enclave may, suggests Jonathan Porter, have something to do with Macao being the furthest outpost of military operations – and the only one left after Portugal lost control of the seas – to be mentioned in Camões' great epic about Vasco da Gama's discovery of the sea route to the Indies. It also legitimizes a presence: rather as if Shakespeare, in another life, had spent time in Hong Kong . . .

Macao had other great exiles. Such as the painter George Chinnery who landed in 1825. He was probably fleeing his harpy of a wife ('the most horrible woman I've ever met', he used to say) as much as his creditors in India. Before him another nomadic poet, the satirist Manuel Maria Barbosa du Bocage (1765–1805) had also sought refuge in Macao. He was a deserter. Because of its nature as a mercantile republic, and because of its geographical position – isolated from both Portugal and China, although in the shadow of the latter, and far from revolutions, wars and invasions – Macao was, from the 1600s until the time of the Cultural Revolution, a land of asylum for oppressed people, refugees and those who had something to escape from. The enclave was initially a shelter for the Chinese: from the first immigrants fleeing the Manchurian conquerors in the 17th century to refugees escaping Maoist China, not forgetting Sun Yat-sen (1866–1925) the 'father' of the 1910 Republic. Born in a charming, simple house in a village in the Xiangshan region, twenty kilometres from Macao, Sun Yat-sen lived in the enclave where for some time he practised as a doctor: he felt safer there than under British sovereignty in Hong Kong. But Macao was also a land of asylum for all nationalities and races: from converted Christian Jews fleeing the Inquisition to refugees from Shanghai after the

Japanese invasion of China in 1937. Following close on their heels, thousands of Chinese landed in Hong Kong and then Macao: when the British colony fell into Japanese hands in 1941, this prompted a fresh exodus towards the Portuguese possession whose authorities decided to use the revenue from taxes on gambling to help the refugees.

At the start of the previous century, the enclave had already welcomed Europeans alarmed by increasingly feverish xenophobia in China. Then White Russians began to arrive in the wake of the 1917 Revolution. One such was George Smirnoff, the perpetual refugee: born in Vladivostok in 1903, he fled with his family from the 1917 Revolution to Harbin in Manchuria, setting off again to escape the Japanese and arriving in Hong Kong where a fresh advance by Japanese armies forced him to move on to Macao.

When the Communists came to power in 1949, there was another Chinese exodus to the enclave. At least 100,000 escaped through Macao. 'Some swam here, others arrived on planks or rafts. There were doctors and technicians, rich and poor among them', recalls Sister Bertha, a Marian Franciscan who looked after them at the time. After 60 years as a missionary, including stints in remote areas of China, where she had arrived at the age of 23, then in Macao and finally in Biafra, she chose to spend the rest of her days in the enclave: 'My life is here, on Chinese soil', she says. Macao, after all, welcomed those poor wretches (the blind and the crippled) who came to beg in its streets after being branded 'useless mouths' in China's 'Great Leap Forward', as well as later on welcoming thousands of freedom swimmers escaping the Cultural Revolution. 'Macao was their last hope,' Father Mario Acquistapace used to say. But in 1966 the Portuguese authorities were forced to yield to Chinese demands and agreed to send the escapees back to Red China. The exodus continued on a clandestine and riskier basis.

Despite submitting to Beijing's orders, Macao remained a place of refuge. For Burmese of Chinese origin, for example, and for certain Jewish and stateless Russians like 'Michael', whom I used to meet at the Hotel Casino Estoril, in the sauna bar he declared to be his 'office'. After practising medicine, trafficking in Shanghai and spying for the British, he ended his days in Macao. An old man with an emaciated face and blue eyes, he would willingly tell his life story but, before it was time to leave, he always made me promise 'not to write any of that down'. Promises should be kept, particularly if they were made in bars. The enclave was also shelter for Fernando the restaurant owner. Dubbed 'the terror of Coloane' for driving like a Formula 1 racing driver, he's run one of the most famous Portuguese restaurants in Macao since 1979. For him as for many others, the enclave was a haven.

Macao's golden age was a bygone one, with the city starting to lose its commercial importance as far back as the 1650s. And yet the ensuing centuries saw some of the finest moments in its history: as a land of exiles. They also saw some of the most sinister, for Macao was central to trafficking in opium and coolies as well as being a playground for every kind of vice. The city has always combined the best with the worst: which accounts for the profound humanity you dimly detected from the moment you set foot there.

A city of transit, a city of refuge, a city of adoption: chance or destiny brought all sorts of men and women to Macao, in pursuit of profit and the conquest of souls. Wandering among the tombs of its cemeteries (Buddhist, Taoist, Catholic, Protestant, Parsee, Muslim), you begin to understand the extent to which its society was a mosaic of races. Unlike the cemeteries for foreigners at Yokohama or Kobe in Japan, where all the outsiders are laid to rest together (grouped by denomination but all in the same area), in a city as racially and culturally mixed as Macao they are separated in death. Each cemetery whispers its history. In the heart of the city, the Catholic cemetery of San Miguel with its Baroque ostentation, its statues of winged angels and women weeping, its busts and marble monuments embellished with coats of arms, tells the story of the great Portuguese and Macanese families: the Mellos, who dominated life in the enclave during the latter part of the 19th century, as well as the Marques and the da Silvas who moved to Macao in the 18th century. The poet Camílio Pessanha was also laid to rest here, as was Ho Yin, the influential banker, whose tomb bears the simple epitaph: 'Patriot and benefactor'.

In the great era of the Cantonese trade (1785–1833), British merchants were joined by Parsees from Bombay and Armenians from Isfahan who hadn't waited for British victory before pushing as far as China and settling in Macao. The Armenian cemetery has disappeared. The Parsee cemetery, built on terraces forming an ampitheatre in a small valley on Guia Hill, used to overlook the sea. It's rather neglected now and the tombs are overgrown. Some of the lots even look vacant, as if to welcome the newly dead. Many of the tombs belong to young men who set off in search of adventure and never came back alive. Others are those of important figures: one monument is dedicated to Pestonjee Cowasjee, who died in 1842, founder of the firm of the same name and William Jardine's Indian opposite number, whose ships ploughed the seas between India and Macao with their cargoes of opium. In the Protestant cemetery, under the frangipani whose fragrant flowers are picked in season by children, the tombs of young British and American sailors and soldiers, men who died from fevers on the far side of the world, are lined up behind one of Sir Winston Churchill's great-uncles: Lord Henry John Spencer Churchill – captain of HMS *Druid* – who died in Macao in 1840. A little further off is a tomb with the simple epitaph *Sacred to the Memory of Thomas Beale*. These laconic words mask a telling destiny of fortunes and misfortunes, with Macao as its theatre.

Thomas Beale was a British subject who arrived in China at the end of the 18th century, to join his brother Daniel, then working for a Cantonese firm. He was seventeen years old. Ostensibly a secretary to the Prussian Consul, the young man revelled in his diplomatic immunity. As foreigners weren't allowed to stay in Canton outside the trading season, he set himself up in Macao, where he was to spend more than 50

The tomb of Thomas Beale, in the Protestant cemetery.

years. He quickly amassed a vast fortune in the opium trade. Thomas Beale soon became one of the richest men in Macao, and his house on the Praia Grande, surrounded by high walls, was the most lavish in the enclave in the 1820s. Its extraordinary exotic garden was renowned for its 2,000 varieties of plants, together with its large aviaries of rare birds, each more magnificent than the last; it offered more sophistication than the exquisite Casa Garden, home to members of the East India Company and the Luis de Camões Museum. Beale intended to go back to England, but a reversal of fortunes decided otherwise. The Canton authorities unexpectedly confiscated the opium cargoes on which he'd drawn a bill of exchange; and when he also became involved in an operation with Miguel de Arriaga, the enclave's unscrupulous judge, Beale, who was used to having Macao at his feet, suddenly found himself unable to meet his financial commitments. Arriaga was unwilling to risk his reputation by exposing the affair, so he 'dropped' Beale. The powerful merchant was declared bankrupt and lost everything. He stayed in Macao, going to live 'outside the walls' in the home of his trusty old comprador. He spent the last years of his life condemned to poverty and oblivion. Mysteriously, he was found dead on a beach in January 1841. Macao's entire foreign community attended his funeral. But the story doesn't end there. A few weeks after Thomas Beale's body was discovered, three fishermen who lived near the shore where he'd been found showed up at the comprador's house with the following tale: several weeks earlier, a foreigner who spoke good Chinese had come to see them. He told them there was a dead man's body on the beach that needed burying. They refused at first, fearing trouble with the authorities. The man was insistent and invoked all the local superstitions linked to death in order to persuade them. His persistence paid off, and they agreed. But as they were preparing to leave for the beach, the stranger said categorically: 'No. Not this evening. You don't bury the dead at night. Tomorrow.' And he left. The next day the fishermen went to the beach. Sure enough, they found the corpse of a fully clothed man. To their amazement, they realized it was the stranger who'd come to see them the night before. They buried him on the spot rather too hastily and, a few weeks later, the corpse was discovered. Since they'd imperfectly acquitted themselves of the task, the fishermen wanted to reimburse the comprador with the money offered them by the foreigner.

Thomas Beale's garden, the agreeable company of young ladies from Britain and America, and George Chinnery's studio were some of Macao's pleasures in the first half of the 19th century, notes the English naturalist George Bennett. A small, open and hospitable world, the eccentric foreign community was largely Anglo-Saxon, particularly during the long periods of hibernation between the trading seasons in Canton: the richest among these new arrivals were supercargoes employed by the East India Company. As well as enjoying a more clement climate than Canton's during the summer months, Macao offered distractions: hunting, fishing, boating trips. And there were plenty of women. 'We have, in Macao, all the elements of a highly civilized society,' wrote Théophile de Ferrière Le Vayer around 1860. A view shared by the lawyer Georges Bousquet, who evokes Macao's elegant society of the same era. This small foreign elite lived on the 'hill' and went from party to party. It comprised influential British, American, Armenian and Indian merchant venturers, as well as eccentric artists like George Chinnery, described by Harriet Low – a young and pretty American who accompanied her merchant uncle to Macao and became the darling of local high society in the early 1830s – in her *Diary* as 'fascinatingly ugly . . . and would have been unbearable if he hadn't been so agreeable'. The Swede Anders Ljungstedt, author of the first history of Macao (1836), was a member of this select society and, like Chinnery, he was laid to rest in the Protestant cemetery. The Americans, British, Dutch and Swedes of the enclave gave the churches a wide berth, but frequented the Pedro V Theatre built in 1859.

The expatriate community included Protestant missionaries who arrived at the beginning of the 19th century, like the Scotsman Robert Morrison who in 1807 was the first to set foot on what was 'Catholic soil'. Treading on Matteo Ricci's territory and anxious to adapt to Chinese customs, this extraordinary character who wore his hair tied in a pigtail contributed to the revival in Chinese studies. As well as being the first translator of Chinese writings and the author of a Sino-English dictionary, he is best known for having forced the Macao authorities to grant Protestants the right to a burial place in the enclave, following the death of his wife from malaria in 1821.

The elite society, with its penchant for showing off, endless meals and intrigues, was also restrictive and petty, and there were those who quickly tired of its appeal as a 'tropical Capua': 'My God, how tedious! Once the ships leave, we've got at least seven month to twiddle our thumbs,' complained the Frenchman François Terrien in the late 18th century. A compatriot of his, the trader Charles de Constant, who was staying in the enclave at the same time, scoffed at 'the handful of European women these Ostrogoths ogle as if they were goddesses, though they have so little education they could be washerwomen for all I care . . .'

Lou Lim Iok garden.

In any case, expatriate community life was nothing more than the 'fluff' of daily life in Macao. Another elite formed during the 19th century, and this time it was Chinese. One of its members was Lou Cheok-chi, originally from Canton, who settled in Macao in around 1860. He too had an enormous house built for himself, complete with pavilions for his nine concubines, and the most beautiful Chinese garden in the enclave, with mountains of rocks, waterfalls, miniature forests, lake and bridges snaking above the lotus lilies. Named after his son Lou Lim Iok, who made it even more extraordinary, the garden is today surrounded by buildings.

Until the 19th century Macao was just a transit city for foreigners and Portuguese from the mainland, and although the Chinese afforded the city its character, its soul lay with the *Macaenses* (Macanese) or 'sons of the land' mentioned earlier.

The oldest well in Macao used to be on the Praça da Fonte do Lilau, on top of Penha Hill: the first navigators who landed in front of A-Ma's Temple climbed the hill behind it to draw water. Legend had it that those who drank the water would never forget Macao, and would either marry there or come

100

back again. The old well has vanished from the square shaded by banyan trees. But who knows? Perhaps there's some truth in the legend that many of those who drank its water founded their line in Macao. There are no more than 25,000 Macanese throughout the world, scattered between Australia, Brazil, Canada and the United States. Ten thousand (barely 3 per cent of the total population) were still living in Macao on the eve of the handover to China.

These 'sons of the land' (*filhos da terra*) who claim Creole identity are the fruit of four centuries of interbreeding. Portuguese, Chinese, Malay, Indian, Japanese, Philippino, British and Dutch blood flows in their veins, as well as black African blood from Mozambique and the Cape. Men with hooked noses and golden skin, women with dumpy Mediterranean bodies but slender shoulders, high cheekbones and oriental eyes are born from a ceaseless crossing of races – and mixing of blood – that dates back to the 17th century. These 'astonishing racial marriages' have given rise to 'one of the greatest experiments in eugenics throughout history' (Rudolf Reis).

At first, women supplied the fresh blood: Malays from Malacca, Indians from Goa and, in smaller numbers, the daughters of Japanese Christian refugees followed by those of Chinese refugees. There were very few European women in Macao before the end of the 18th century, so the men took servants or slaves as mistresses or wives. Facilitated by liberal values, these unions were also encouraged by Afonso de Albuquerque, who sought to legitimize cohabitation through baptism and marriage from the outset of the conquests in order to lay down roots for the Portuguese presence. These mixed unions formed the basis of the region's multi-racial society: unlike Hong Kong where, under British domination, such reprobate partnerships stayed hidden. A century after the first Portuguese arrived in Macao, a population with unusual morphological features began to emerge in the initial stages of a Creole, hybrid, trans-national culture.

For a long time there were more women than men in Macao. At the beginning of the 17th century the town was described by missionaries as 'a city of women'. Many were orphans born from unions with servants. They were taken in by the Santa Casa de Misericórdia, given a Christian education and placed with rich families. Others became prostitutes. Such as Martha Merop, who lived from the late 1700s until the early 1800s, and whose full-length portrait hangs in the grand chamber in the Santa Casa de Misericórdia. Austin Coates dedicated a novel to the legend of this enigmatic woman, mistress to an Englishman in the East India Company, and had his heroine say she felt 'neither Portuguese nor Chinese'. The novel's title, *City of Broken Promises*, alludes to the promises of marriage Europeans used to make their mistresses before, more often than not, abandoning them with their children. Martha Merop was sold as a prostitute at the age of thirteen, and lived with her lover Thomas van Merop for fifteen years. He departed from Macao without her, but bequeathed her his fortune and his name. Martha launched herself in business and became the richest woman in South China, as well as the Santa Casa's most generous donor.

During the 18th century, the wives and mistresses of the Portuguese (or Asian-Portuguese) in Macao were Eurasian (*metizinhas*) and then Chinese. But the beginning of the 19th century saw the arrival of the first European women, prompting a counter movement: some *filhos da terra* started marrying white women. The population's diverse roots afford the geographical confetti of Macao a unique place in the history of humanity.

Across the centuries an intermittent process of cultural mixing took place in Macao, by assimilating, contaminating, transforming, adapting and reacting with the disparate European, Chinese, Malaysian and Indian elements in a new cultural mosaic. This blend was often beneficial to Macao's merchants when they were competing with other Europeans: the Macanese possessed physical, linguistic and cultural affinities with the native peoples, as well as an ability to adapt which their competitors lacked. Macao's cultural hybrid is reflected in a style of architecture showing Lusitanian–Asian influences. But you can also find an expression of aesthetic blending in the watercolours of a 19th-century artist such as Marciano Baptista. Baptista attended George Chinnery's school and was probably the best Macanese artist of his era, a representative of the school of painting that married foreign and local influences, as it developed in Macao and later on in Canton and Japan as they became aware of Western-style artistic representation.

Has the hybrid nature of Macanese culture forged a strong identity? And in what way is it different from those Creole cultures that emerged from different cross-combinations throughout the former Portuguese Empire from Cape Verde all the way to Timor, and including Goa and Malacca?

The Macanese tend to emphasize their Portuguese roots and underplay the Asian or Chinese part of their heritage. But mainland Portuguese ethnocentrism is, at the same time, interpreted as a form of ostracism by many of those who think of themselves as 'the Portuguese of Asia'. When Macao's golden age came to an end in the 17th century with the closure of the 'Japan route' and the loss of Malacca, the *casados* (Portuguese who had settled and married there) found themselves isolated both from Portugal because of its geographical distance and from China despite its proximity. In spite of their racial polymorphism and their affinities with the local culture, the Macanese remained 'barbarian' like the Europeans in the eyes of the Chinese. Aware they belonged to neither country, the Macanese still claimed Portuguese nationality.

There is no definition for 'Macanese'. Is it reserved for those of mixed blood or does it refer to anyone born in Macao? We don't even know how many Macanese there are. 'To be Macanese is a state of mind: we're the children of a love affair between Asia and the West and we're proud of our mixed blood', says Henrique Rodrigues de Senna Fernandes, a barrister and novelist whose family tree can be traced back two and a half centuries. Portuguese, Chinese and Malaysian blood flows in his veins. 'We don't have any international heroes and our history is provincial compared to that of major countries, but our way of living and thinking goes back three centuries. We've built our own "world" here. Without the Macanese, Macao is just another Chinese city like so many others.' Henrique Rodrigues de Senna Fernandes has written several novels set in the Macao of his childhood.

The native Creole culture was largely shaped by women. The historian C. R. Boxer observes that, though far from being matriarchal, Macanese society was less misogynous than Portuguese society. The women of Macao seem to have enjoyed more freedom and power in the heart of the community than Portuguese or Chinese women at the time: they could 'inherit the seal' – in other words, their father's business. Women were the guardians of Macanese identity as expressed in its cuisine, in attire more suited to the climate and in its patois. The cuisine in particular remains a living testimony to Macao's Creole culture. Its recipes borrow little from China, adapting instead the flavours of India and Malaysia to the Western palate. Gastronomy in Macao combines the great traditions of hospitality from these countries: the *chá gordo* (a lavish tea whose presentation is rivalled only by the range of delicacies on offer) highlights the extraordinary culinary saga that gave rise to Macanese cuisine, allied as it is to the ostentatious and typically Latin tastes of Macao's great families.

Above all, women have been responsible for preserving one of the most important elements in Macanese culture: *patoá* (the local dialect). Macao's social life is divided into two linguistic worlds: Cantonese and Portuguese. These are not strictly ethnic worlds, since someone may have access to both worlds provided they have the requisite linguistic skills. A third and far more contained world, now in the process of disappearing, was that of 'Macao's gentle *patois*'. This is a relic from the time when Portuguese was the trading *língua franca* in Asia, and the language had to be simplified in order to make it more accessible for native populations. It was also enriched by elements from local languages. The Macao dialect is mainly derived from the dialect of Malacca (*kristang*). After that city fell into Dutch hands, the Portuguese emigrated towards Flores and Java and were then pushed back as far as Macao. *Kristang*, which had already reached Macao, care of women from Malacca, evolved into a language of its own in the enclave: a mixture of old Portuguese and phrases from spoken Malay, Indian and Chinese. 'A language both supple and subtle in its play of words and richness of poetic expression', says Henrique Rodrigues de Senna Fernandes.

Until the end of the 19th century, women from the great Macanese families affected not to speak Cantonese and conversed only in patois. But this use of dialect declined abruptly when Lisbon decreed that all administration should be carried out in Portuguese. The decline was rapid because Macanese patois had never sought recognition as a language in its own right, or been a vehicle for resistance, as *kristang* became for a minority in Malacca after the city fell into Dutch hands, and as was more strongly the case in Cape Verde, where the local dialect is almost a national language. Being intermediaries between the Chinese and Portuguese (or Europeans) made it all the more difficult for the Macanese to define themselves. Today, a Macanese elite educated in Portuguese is trying to encourage an artificial patois revival in the theatre, but ordinary people are reluctant to admit they speak the local dialect – often they're no longer fluent, anyway – for fear of losing face. The Macanese seem to have lost confidence in their cultural identity.

They form a complex and diverse microcosm within undefined parameters. Ostracized both by the Chinese and the mainland Portuguese who tend to look down their noses at them, theirs is a closed and conservative community of practising Catholics, so strongly hierarchical that segregation occurs even within its own bosom: 'We know too much about each family; and grudges get passed down from generation to generation', says one Macanese. The Macanese community is also one where class divisions are strongly felt: there's a sort of local aristocracy formed by big families descended from powerful merchant stock (*mestiços brancos*: half-whites), who tend to set themselves apart from the blue-collar workers, often employed in administrative jobs, who make up the community's middle and lower classes. The *Português-de-pataca* (the 'pataca Portuguese' – named after the local currency), referring to those Chinese who sought to procure themselves Portuguese ancestry in the 19th century by buying up pretentious names from unscrupulous parish employees, are also looked down on.

The Macanese community has suffered several setbacks since the 1850s. The first of these, as we've already seen, was the order from Portugal for all administration to be carried out in the national language; this diktat cost the patois its prestige and usefulness as a *língua franca*: those wishing to maintain their reputation and play a part in the machinery of power had to speak Portuguese. Business was – and still is – conducted in Chinese or English. So patois was relegated from the public domain to that of the family. Its withdrawal was further accentuated in the wake of the Opium Wars, when many Portuguese and Macanese emigrated to Hong Kong, where they were among the city's first builders (they constructed churches and schools) and formed the framework for its first banks, including the Hong Kong & Shanghai Bank. The 'Club Lusitano', which opened in 1866, was the top venue for the British colony's shows and galas. And it was the Portuguese and Macanese who began developing the district between Tsimshatsui and Kowloon in the early stages of the 20th century. Others emigrated to Shanghai at around the same time. But after the Japanese invasion of China and following the fall of Hong Kong and finally the Communist seizure of power, they flooded back to Macao, only to emigrate again from there to Australia and the United States.

In the enclave itself, the Macanese were progressively superseded towards the late 1800s by powerful Chinese families who controlled the enclave's economy. Portugal's prestige was later damaged by the Cultural Revolution, and the Macanese sense of belonging was further unhinged when the Governor was forced to issue a public apology for having opened fire on the demonstrators. In the 1980s the influx of new arrivals from Portugal, attracted by the region's dynamism and the prospect of lucrative business before the handover, proved another blow to the Macanese. This new 'elite', who thought it could take advantage of the last days under Portuguese administration in order to make a fast buck, scorned the 'locals', whether Macanese or Chinese, thereby bringing the two communities closer together, in a process begun with mixed marriages in the 19th century. As the time for the handover was drawing near, the Macanese became increasingly Sinified. Unlike their parents, the young generation of 'new Macanese' feel closer to their Chinese contemporaries, whose roots lie in the region of Canton, than to the Portuguese. They're driven by the same frenetic urge to make money, they prefer karaoke to fado and speak a version of Cantonese peppered with Portuguese expressions. But the 'petty' Macanese with low-ranking admin-istrative jobs are bitter at being replaced by young Chinese, and find themselves torn between two options, both synonymous with worry and uncertainty: should they stay or leave?

Ten years ago, at the Solmar café-restaurant, not far from the Praia Grande, everyone knew everyone else. Out on the terrace, Macanese regulars would indulge in endless political chat and gossip about the rumours doing the rounds in town. Today, the establishment's been renovated and there are now just one or two tables in the air-conditioned main room where Macanese sit. They are orphans of history. As Graciete Batalha writes, they know they no longer belong to Portugal but they're not Chinese either. The Solmar used to be the barometer of local humour. Today it's glum, as if the rainy season will never end.

The Avenida Almeida Ribeiro.

Vices

In the racket of the smoke-filled gambling den, the frail outline of an old woman so small that the table she's sitting behind cuts her off at chest level, appears to be the still centre of a painting displaying a crowd of male faces around her; some stand next to her, leaning on their elbows, others keep in the background behind her chair, jostling and leaning over her shoulder at intervals to place a bet. The old woman is unmistakably an *amah* (servant), with her sallow face wrinkled and wizened like an old apple, her hair pulled tightly back into a bun and her Chinese black jacket with its threadbare officer's collar. Everyone present in the room is Chinese. Mostly men and a handful of women, they're all simply dressed. They are port workers and blue-collar employees: sailors, fishermen, stevedores, factory workers, shopkeepers. Many wear faded blue overalls frayed at the wrist and caps or beaten-up hats on their heads. Their social standing is betrayed by hollow faces, open shirts exposing scrawny chests, muscular forearms and swollen fingers. Their feverish eyes are riveted to the baize, and the small entrance notice advising clients they should 'only bet what you can afford to lose' seems laughable. They're here in the hope of a lucky break, ready to stake everything from a day's to a week's wages. The floor is strewn with cigarette butts and discarded papers, and in the corners people clear their throats over metal spittoons filled with sand. The sweet-and-sour smell of sweat and smoke hangs in the air.

The old woman keeps both hands firmly under the table. The right one appears to throw down a few red notes on the green baize when the croupier calls the stakes, before quickly disappearing under the table again. The left stays on top of a newspaper folded in four on her lap, from which she extracts Hong Kong dollars one at a time or sometimes in fistfuls, meticulously counting them out without looking down. An hour later she's still there, unwavering, her eyes fixed on the croupier's hands as he begins counting the porcelain pieces using chopsticks.

Fan-tan is an old Chinese game. Wearing a white open shirt that's seen better days, the croupier neatly turns over a silver bowl with the chips piled up inside it. Then he slides the bowl over to the side, raises it and deftly begins to subtract the chips in fours. The outcome of the betting depends on how many are left in the final subtraction: one, two, three or four? Even or odd? Sighs and exclamations follow: *'fat-la, fat-la'* ('our luck's turning'). Expressionless, the croupier gathers up the stakes and dryly throws the notes folded in four towards the winners (cash replaced chips in fan-tan some time ago). Next, he places other notes in small baskets that are tied to a cord and whisked up to the balcony-level overlooking the table. Undemonstrative as ever, the croupier slurps a mouthful of tea that's been infusing in a porcelain cup with a lid, before filling the silver bowl again and shaking it. Soon, notes are once more flying over the table.

The floating casino of the Macao Palace, anchored along the quayside of the Inner Harbour, has, like the Kam Pek on the corner of the Rua Caldeira nearby, with its three floors of seedy gaming rooms and threadbare carpets, long preserved the ambience of the apocryphal 'gaming hell'. No ceremony or croupier in smoking jacket here. Its clientele were originally blue-collar workers. And the games played were mainly Chinese, like fan-tan or dai-sui (big-little) in which three die are handled under a glass bell by the croupier, who was as often as not female. The Macao Palace, which opened in 1962, was an enormous barge with three decks decorated 'Chinese style' in luridly bad taste. It boasted overly ornate gangways lined with yellow guard-rails, while the barge itself was decorated with golden dragons coiled around sky-blue columns at the entrance, which was in turn surmounted by a flying roof and flanked by gaudy phoenixes. The wreath of lights from the Macao Palace would shimmer from the far end of the Avenida Almeida Ribeiro as soon as night fell. The players were spread out between the split-level fan-tan rooms and those with roulette and baccarat tables. Along the harbour front nearby, under the arcades of houses with decrepit façades eaten away by the damp, the lights would shine from the pawnbroker shops that never shut. People down on their luck would pawn whatever they had (a watch, jewels, a camera) in the hope their luck would turn and they would be able to recoup them. The old Macao Palace has since been replaced by concrete barges filled with slot machines. And the Kam Pek has closed down.

As you leave the Macao Palace and cross the harbour, you pass one of the old port hotels, the Grand Kuoc Chai; also decrepit, it's notorious for the accounts settled there by sub-machine-gun since it began life in the 1930s. In the dark surrounding streets the stench of urine and rotten fish mingles with the smell of silt from the docks. In silent alleys your footsteps ring out and shifty figures disappear, swallowed by the shadows. Women from the neighbouring Chinese provinces, young girls mostly, loiter in halos of light, hoping to lure passers-by into one of the small seedy hotels along the Rua de Virtudes. The area around the Inner Harbour is best known for the Rua da Felicidade. An ordinary narrow street rising up towards the Christian town, today it's become a tourist spot famous for the glittering lights of its restaurants and for its renovated houses. This district was the crucible of Macao's underworld.

The 'city in the name of God in China' was a citadel scarred by heresy: the Church never succeeding in wiping out 'sin'. A city of priests in black oblong hats and nuns in white cornets, of women dressed from head to toe in black scurrying to mass with their faces hidden beneath long shawls clutched at the chest, it was also a languorous city of base delights: of stupor, opium and gambling. As dusk fell, the prudish and sleepy

Christian city of Macao gave way, in the maze of streets lit by lanterns in the Chinese district, to Macao the city of sin. In the 1750s a Franciscan described the enclave as a place of 'robbery, trickery, gambling, drunkenness, and every kind of vice'. The Church regularly showed concern about the number of women who gave themselves up to prostitution. But nothing changed. The surplus female population, the comings and goings of ships and the nature of Macao as a transit city combined with the decline in trade to encourage a loosening of moral codes. In his summary of impressions from 18th-century travellers, Louis Dermigny observes how the high proportion of women, both free and slaves, widows and those claiming that status, wives for a day or a season and prostitutes of every origin and colour afforded the city a pernicious atmosphere. The French merchant Charles Constant, nicknamed 'Constant the Chinaman' on account of his lengthy visits to the Middle Kingdom between 1779 and 1793, wrote in his *Mémoires* that Macao's population was two-thirds female. And in the 18th century the enclave became a prolific marketplace for women sold in Mozambique and the Zambezi valley. 'The Portuguese consider the buying up of Chinese children in order to raise them in the Christian religion as a pious deed . . . their preference is for girls because they are more likely to be able to keep themselves through prostitution; some have made a fortune and amply reimbursed their adoptive parents for the cost of raising them,' writes Constant. Foreigners who spent their winters in Macao between the trading seasons in Canton had nothing to do, according to our author, except kill time, and the majority of them 'squandered their energies'.

Life in the Chinese part of the city barely features in pre-19th-century chronicles of Macao left by Europeans, and when it does the focus is mostly on the Rua da Felicidade and its 'flower houses' or places of pleasure. In China, and, following suit, in Japan, the word 'flower' is a euphemism used to denote prostitutes: people used to talk about 'districts of flowers and willows' meaning the geisha districts in Japanese cities, while the term 'flower boats' referred to the floating brothels in Canton. The Portuguese authorities turned a blind eye to what was going on in the Chinese district, leaving the control of the *demi-monde* in the hands of natives and a few Macanese. Most of the girls were orphans or abandoned children sold by their parents to brothel-keepers charged with teaching them the map of pleasure and the art of attraction. The Rua da Felicidade was lined with two-storey houses. The girls would sit in front of the wide first-floor windows while the old madams waited by the red lanterns of the main entrance, smoking their cigars.

Travellers tell tales of how late the district would stir. It shook off its torpor in the afternoon, to the first drifting melodies and nostalgic songs. But the Rua da Felicidade wasn't always a street of common prostitutes. The girls there used to be educated, they knew how to play a musical instrument and were skilled in the arts of dancing and conversation. Their bearing and self-restraint would secure an establishment's reputation, and they were selective when it came to clients. Seductive prowess enabled the most beautiful to became the mistresses of rich merchants. But the majority were older and less educated, and they were sold to their madam for life, with no future other than the tragic decline common to all pleasure district girls, when the 'flowers' they once were begin to fade.

Another type of unceremonious prostitution existed at the port: that of the 'wild whores', as the girls of the street were called in Shanghai. They hustled for sailors and fishermen and would carry out their business on a piece of matting in a dark corner.

Opium dens and factories where the paste for smoking was fabricated and stockpiled could also be found around the district of the Inner Harbour. Down by the docks, on the corner of the Praça da Ponte e Horta and the Rua das Lorchas, you can still see one of those factories: a small one-storey building in colonial style, sand-coloured with dark brown shutters and doors that haven't opened for years. Old men play at mahjong under its arcades. If we're to believe Charles Constant, who stayed in Macao in the late 18th century, well before the offensive by European traffickers, the enclave was already the scene of a considerable opium trade, mostly for the consumption of local inhabitants. The smoking dens and factories where opium was legally prepared (licences were issued by the authorities) were, together with the brothels, another of Macao's 'tourist' attractions, duly listed in *The Tourists' Guide to Canton, The West River and Macao* published in 1898. The Conde d'Arnoso, a Portuguese diplomat who was part of the delegation sent to Beijing to sign the first Sino-Portuguese treaty and who stayed in Macao in 1887, describes the smoking dens as 'clubs'. They occupied large houses with thin wood-carved walls dividing a suite of small cubicles, each furnished with two beds where the clients lay down and inhaled the drug, their eyes half-closed. 'The 'opium farm' (one of the factories where the smoking paste was made), 'is one of Macao's assets', wrote the young Frenchman Gérard Weulersse, who visited the enclave in 1900.

> Three hundred workers are involved making the precious narcotic and the factory has the only steam pump in Macao. The opium arrives from India in balls the size of coconuts . . . It's one of the colony's principal and most lucrative exports: a small box of opium worth six piastres in Macao is worth three times that amount in *San Francisco*.

The Englishman Archie Bell observed in 1917 that he saw 'more opium' produced in ten minutes 'than one would imagine there to be in all the world'. In 1938 the United States raised the question of Macao's production and traffic of opium before the League of Nations. But the trade in the drug, legal or otherwise, was an important source of revenue for the authorities and it carried on.

Gambling has provided Macao with most of its income since the early 20th century. First practised in the Rua da Felicidade, it was linked to opium dens from the outset: dives often had beds in their back rooms for smoking purposes.

With the demise of the traffic in coolies, Macao sank into a new era of decadence and poverty. Having dealt a deathblow to the enclave by creating Hong Kong, Victorian Britain then offered it the poisoned chalice of gambling. Shocked by the moral depravity of its new colony (23 brothels, 400 prostitutes, 24 opium dens and several gambling joints), the British Crown imposed harsh measures against opium and gambling, but prostitution carried on: the old district of Wanchai – described by Richard Mason in his novel *The World of Suzie Wong* – and now in the grip of modernization, was for decades the haunt of sailors of every nationality as well as American soldiers on leave from Vietnam. In the early 1870s there were just a few secret gambling joints in Hong Kong. But gambling had already begun to flourish in Macao. It came into its own following the ban in Canton in 1911.

Gambling wasn't a new pastime in Macao. But the 'gambling hell' of concessionary Shanghai was infinitely more turbulent than that of the enclave. Together with opium, foreigners had introduced a whole gamut of gambling that would intoxicate Shanghai for more than half a century. Not that the superstitious Chinese had waited for the arrival of foreigners to become inveterate gamblers: Father Huc, a missionary who arrived in China in 1847, blamed the Middle Kingdom's rampant poverty on several evils, with gambling second only to the neglect of power. 'The laws of the Kingdom forbid gambling; but the legislation has been so overwhelmed by public practice that China today resembles a enormous gambling joint', he wrote. According to the good Father, the Chinese were driven to the worst excesses by their passion, including gambling away their own wives and the fingers off their hands. 'It's common to see large families suddenly slip into the most appalling poverty after several rounds of cards or dice.'

Gambling developed in tandem in Shanghai and Macao. The managers of the Shanghai joints were often Macanese or Chinese from Macao, like the Cantonese Liang Pei who, in 1927, after making a fortune from the Portuguese enclave's gambling habits, opened two gigantic casinos in the French concession with 50 rooms open round the clock. His establishments were toppled a few years later by the '181', the street number of an even bigger and more luxurious casino (also built in the French concession).

Gambling began to assume a real importance in the enclave from the 1850s onwards. As well as numerous gambling joints, lotteries remained one of the great popular pastimes. Even the Santa Casa de Misericórdia had its own lottery. Simple folk had a particular penchant for a Cantonese game: a special lottery called the Assembly of Flowers, where you had to guess which out of 36 famous historical characters would be drawn. Placing the game under the protection of Guan Yin (a divinity of Compassion) meant the players were further taken advantage of. The lower and devout classes in Macao, especially women who thought they'd be favoured by the divinity for surrendering to increasingly wild superstitious practices that sometimes led to terrible tragedies, were ravaged by this rampant trickery controlled by the underworld and banned several times in China.

The authorities turned a blind eye to the gambling joints, or else made sure their lax approach was duly rewarded. Then, as the city's economic situation continued to decline, they recognized the profits they stood to gain from gambling if it was regulated and legalized in return for taxation.

The first licences were granted in the 1850s: the Macao government was in need of revenue when the city became an administrative entity together with Timor and Sohor, and Governor Isidoro Francisco Guimarães decided to regulate and tax gambling. In 1886 there were sixteen gambling rooms in the Inner Harbour district and along the Rua da Felicidade. They constituted a tourist attraction and were listed as such by the *The Tourists' Guide* of 1898. Twenty years previously, the Comte de Beauvoir was already talking about Macao as the 'Celestial Empire's Monaco'. He described gambling establishments frequented by rich Chinese, with croupiers who were 'patriarchs with white pigtails, beards of four waxed hairs and inordinately long nails presiding over a bank flooded by hundreds of players'. In 1873 the British review *Graphic* published an astonishing illustration depicting a group of players gathered around a fan-tan table: two foreigners, some pig-tailed Chinamen and a young woman with a folded fan in one hand apparently receiving her winnings in the other. Another illustration showed the first floor gallery with men and women leaning over the guard-rail and watching the table below while the little baskets containing the bets were raised and lowered. The young Frenchman Gérard Weulersse described the Casa de Jogo, one of Macao's famous gambling joints in 1900:

> You climb a rather dirty wooden staircase to reach a room that's fairly well-lit but bare and cramped. It's essentially a spectators' gallery: a wide circular opening gives onto the gaming room proper situated below [whose] big table [is] covered not with the usual green baize but with fine yellow matting. The croupier deals the stakes and settles the accounts with prodigious agility: his hands never stop, nor does his tongue; he sweats profusely, and his open jacket reveals his bare brown chest. The players' poise is also striking. There is an anxious attentiveness, with torsos leaning in, eyes wide open, but not a twitch of the hand or a word to pass their lips.

From 1934, the system of granting licences separately to each gambling establishment was abolished and replaced by a monopoly. The gambling monopoly was awarded to a syndicate, Tai Xing and Co. Most gambling houses at the time were under the thumb of the O family, which had an extraordinary history. After coming into a hefty fortune from his father, O Iec Tong (O Loc) had opened up gambling houses along the Rua da Felicidade in the late 19th century. His father, O Leun Sec (O Hei Kung), was a coolie from Fujian. Like thousands of other poor devils, he had set off to work in Malaysia's rubber and rice plantations. He was looked kindly on by the owner, who made him first his steward and then heir to his plantations. He returned to Canton a rich man and became a member of the Thirteen Hong (a guild of businesses specializing in foreign trade). His monopoly of the rice trade in South China enabled him to acquired a large house with a garden giving onto the Praia Grande as his holiday home. This house went on to become the O family residence, and the family became one of the most prestigious Chinese families in Macao. As a child at the end of the 1940s, Irene O, great-great-granddaughter of O Iec Tong, remembers being frightened of crossing her ancestors' portrait gallery in the big house and recalls her grandmother, the haughty daughter of a Mandarin from the Canton region, forbidding her from socializing with Macanese children.

After O Iec Tong's death in 1913, the empire passed to his son, O Tin Tai. Married to the daughter of a Mandarin, he enjoyed the high life and begun smoking opium at the age of twenty. He rarely ventured outside his huge house on the Praia Grande, living on smoked ham and honey washed down with brandy. O Tin Tai's evenings were devoted to opium. Meanwhile, the gambling empire was managed by Kou Ho Neng, one of his father's trustworthy men. A street still bears the name of this Macao legend. When O Tin Tai died, the family decided to make their gambling business over to their manager, who in turn gave control to his bodyguard, Fu Tak Iam. A giant from North China and a colourful character to boot, he'd arrived in Canton in the entourage of a gambling-joint manager. Fu turned out to be a real shark and ruled over the gambling scene for 24 years. He was superstitious and thought that red brought luck to the players while white and green favoured the 'bank'. So red was banned from his gambling rooms. His large house, which now lies empty on the Praia Grande, is entirely sea-green. It consists of two substantial buildings in colonial style with verandahs and a patio: Fu and his family lived in one, his favourite concubine in the other.

The Central Hotel.

Fu opened the first grand casino in 1928 in the Central Hotel, where all the employees wore green-and-white uniforms. The hotel still stands on the Avenida Almeida Ribeiro, its sign lit up with huge ideograms. It's rather run down now, and lost its casino on Fu's death. But at the time, the Central was the most modern hotel in the city, as well as being the tallest building (at twelve storeys). In addition to the gambling rooms, it boasted a cinema and a cabaret where you could play fan-tan while dancing: hostesses would record the bets in a counterfoil book and the results were posted on a large illuminated board. The Central deposed another hotel, the romantic Riviera on the corner of the Avenida Almeida Ribeiro and the Praia Grande. Built in the colonial style, its wide verandahs giving onto the bay, Italian furniture and orchestra playing waltzes at teatime, afforded it an elegance that survived until 1971.

When the Central opened, gambling became big business in Macao and just about the only means of making money. It also triggered resentment. The hotel was the target of bomb attacks on several occasions, and Fu Tak Iam himself. Fu, who'd become fabulously wealthy (he owned shipping companies, buildings and businesses), was kidnapped in February 1946 in Kun Iam Temple. He liked to go there of an afternoon, to smoke opium in an outbuilding with the pagoda's superior. When the ransom didn't arrive quickly enough, the kidnappers dispatched one of his ears to his family, who paid out an astronomical sum for the time. The intermediary who carried the ransom to Hong Kong was the banker Ho Yin, who went on to become one of Beijing's men in the enclave. Fu was released and gave up smoking at the Pagoda. Seven years later his son was also kidnapped. This time the kidnappers weren't dealing with his family but with Fu himself. They observed the sinister ritual of sending him one of his son's ears, but Fu refused to pay, reasoning that he had enough male heirs. It was the son's mother, one of Fu's concubines, who got the money together and paid for his release.

No light has ever been shed on the abduction of Fu senior, and the motives were probably more than criminal. The case exposes the shady world that held sway in Macao during and after the Second World War. As a neutral country, the enclave was encircled by the Japanese after the seizure of Canton and Hong Kong and became a lair for gangsters, as well as spies of every nationality and *femmes fatales* arriving with the influx of refugees. Although Macao went through a tough year in 1942 (famine and a cholera epidemic), the pernicious atmosphere of a city outside the combat zone reigned throughout the War: people were dying of hunger in the streets and there were even cases of cannibalism, according to Mgr Teixeira, but the cabarets where hostesses wore silk dresses slit up the thigh were, along with the gambling rooms, packed until dawn. Those with the means got high on life as if there was no tomorrow. Gangsters were also spawned in this frivolous and despairing world.

The leader of the group that had kidnapped the 'king of gambling' was arrested. Lei Peng Su was one of the real rogues of that era. A Kuomintang member, he came to Macao in 1944 to

assassinate another 'scoundrel': the leader of the Wong Kong
Kit gang who worked for the Japanese. His bid failed, but not
before shoot-outs in the style of Chicago during the Prohibition
years had taken place inside the Grand Kuoc Chai Hotel.
According to Mgr Teixeira, Wong Kong Kit and his wife were
Macao's 'Bonnie and Clyde'. Wong travelled around in two
cars with eight bodyguards on the running boards armed with
submachine-guns; the verandahs of his office on the Avenida
Coronel Mesquita were protected by sandbags, and a heavy
machine-gun had been installed on the roof. Officially, he was
in charge of the city's rice provisions from Japanese-occupied
Canton, but he was actually working for the Japanese secret
services. On the eve of Japan's capitulation he secretly fled
Macao, hidden in a crate. Arrested on an island to the west of
Hong Kong and extradited to Macao, he was shot down as he
tried to escape from the wagon he'd been travelling in – and
whose door had opportunely been left open.

But back to gambling and trafficking. By the time the War
was over, Macao's reputation as the 'most depraved city in the
world' was sealed. The myth had in some ways been forged in
1939 by Jean Delannoy's film, *Macao, L'enfer du jeu* with Erich
von Stroheim (in the Portuguese version, Macao disappeared
from the title), and its seamy side was captured in another film,
Macao, by Josef von Sternberg (director of *Shanghai-Express*) and
Nicolas Ray. An example of *film noir* if ever there was one, star-
ring Jane Russell and Robert Mitchum, it came out in 1952 but
didn't appear in Portugal for another 30 years. James Bond
author Ian Fleming also helped clinch Macao's reputation
when he wrote in 1959 in *The Sunday Times* that the Central
Hotel was 'the least recommendable place on earth'. The writer
even based the character of Goldfinger on one of Macao's
shady underworld figures: Pedro José Lobo. Lobo, born in
Timor of mixed Malay, Chinese and Portuguese blood, fancied
himself as a composer and always kept a Filipino by his side to
write down the tunes he used to sing. Before the War he'd
headed the commission charged with administering the legal

opium trade (and therefore the trafficking) before becoming president of the refugee support committee when Hong Kong fell into Japanese hands. After the War the 'enigmatic doctor Lobo', as Fleming called him, was, together with Ho Yin, the most powerful figure in Macao's shadows. Portugal wasn't a signatory of the Bretton Woods monetary agreements (1944) linking most currencies to the gold standard. Quick to recognize the financial implications for Macao, Lobo and his banker friend launched themselves in the gold trade. The precious metal was worth 35 dollars an ounce on the international market but 50 in China, where those with the means were buying up ingots as a future investment because they sensed time was up for the Kuomintang . . . and Lobo and Ho banked hefty dividends along the way. So Macao went from being a nerve centre for opium trafficking to one for gold, with the same man as its maestro.

The gold would arrive by seaplanes from Amsterdam and Mexico, whereupon it was dispatched in junks. Millions of dollars worth of gold ounces passed through the enclave in this way . . . with Communist China taking over from wealthy Chinese individuals as a major gold investor. Macao was also an important base for espionage and trafficking (notably in gold) by North Koreans, before that country was semi-bankrupted.

The establishments on the Rua da Felicidade had already shut down, but their activities continued in hotel massage parlours and saunas. As for gambling, it was placed under the control the Sociedade de Turismo e Diversos de Macao (STDM) headed by Stanley Ho, who developed Western games (roulette, baccarat) and organized hydrofoils from Hong Kong to attract players. He also opened up new establishments, such as the Macao Palace and Hotel Casinos Estoril and Lisboa. Stanley Ho had the model of concessionary Shanghai in his head: a city boasting the greatest gambling 'temples', where you could bet on anything from horses and greyhounds to the Basque game of pelota. Macao soon boasted all this, and continues to run popular and lucrative lotteries. Not a gambling city in the region (in the Philippines, Indonesia, South Korea and Malaysia) can hold a candle to this Asian Las Vegas.

Who exactly is 'Dr Stanley Ho', whose name was given to one of the new avenues built on reclaimed land along the Praia Grande? 'Handsome as luck', 'slippery as chance'. The character of this slender-framed, elegantly insouciant 'dandy of the highroad', who transformed the 'gambling hell' into a business that provides Macao with more than half its revenue and Beijing with a sizeable nest egg on the side, hasn't lacked for descriptions. Born into a rich Hong Kong family in 1921, Stanley Ho is of English, Portuguese and Chinese extraction. His cousin was one of the leading figures of the British Colony: Sir Robert Ho Tung (already mentioned with reference to his attractive house on the Santo Agostinho *piazzetta*, which he gave to Macao). But it was as a refugee fleeing the Japanese that the young Stanley Ho arrived in Macao in 1941 with a few dollars in his pocket: his family had been ruined by the War and bad investments. Ho started trafficking using a junk on behalf of a Hong Kong businessman, and, crucially, married the daughter of one of Macao's leading lawyers. After the War, he returned to Hong Kong and launched himself in property, the rice trade and stock-market speculation. He made serious sums of money. In the early 1960s, following the death of Fu, Ho decided to take over the gambling industry in Macao and embarked on a tightly fought battle against Fu's heirs. He travelled to Lisbon, increased promises to government, used his wife's connections for all they were worth, set up a company of local stakeholders and walked away with the invitation from the Portuguese authorities to tender for the gambling monopoly. Ho was the smallest shareholder in the company he'd formed: behind him were the powerful Hong Kong businessman Henry Fok, the mixed-race Malaysian Teddy Yip, and, most importantly, Yip Hon, a man in the shadows, who set all the wheels in motion. Yip was a professional gambler and high-flying character in the Macanese underworld, and he knew how to 'listen to the dice'; in other words, he was an expert on gambling and its environment. The same couldn't be said for his colleagues. He had started gambling as an adolescent in Canton. Then he worked for Fu and opened a casino in Shanghai. Henry Fok was the man who put up the money. Born into a poor family of Hong Kong boat people, Fok had been a stevedore, a coolie, a blacksmith and a grocer before making a fortune in smuggled medicines in China. Regarded as a 'patriotic capitalist' by Beijing and president of the Chinese Chamber of Commerce in the British Colony, Fok was the first leading businessman to invest in the People's China in the early 1970s. Stanley Ho brought with him the Macanese knowledge and connections of his family-in-law. He made his mark as the man in charge of gambling when he closed the doors of his casinos to the Red Guard during the Cultural Revolution. Then he set about ousting Yip Hon, who retired in 1975.

The STDM became a 'state within a state' and the Hotel Casino Lisboa a city within a city. A monument of architectural kitsch, the Lisboa prefigured the way Macao would go 30 years later. Round and honey-coloured with white mouldings like whipped-cream flourishes on a cake, it rises up from what used to be the Praia Grande like a First Communion cake: 'the children's tea-party of gambling', you could say. But its shape is more symbolic than just an architectural fad. The circular building represents a cage imprisoning the gamblers . . . Yet the cage isn't entirely closed, as can be smoothly pointed out in the hotel's reception. The Lisboa was built on the basis of Chinese geomancy: the building represents the head of a dragon whose tail is symbolized by the bridge linking Macao to Taïpa. The geomancer who suggested the architecture of the main entrance confirms that it represents the head of an enormous bat supposed to grab money (the animal also brings good luck because it is pronounced *fuk* in Cantonese, in the same way as the word for happiness).

The Lisboa now boasts 700 bedrooms, with a new building adjacent to the first. More than just a hotel, it's a casino with

The Hotel Lisboa at night.

bedrooms whose gambling rooms operate around the clock. The gamblers sometimes arrive in groups of three or four, paying for just one bedroom and taking it in turns to sleep. The roulette balls never stop jiggling, and the cards and dice, handled by female croupiers with purple uniforms and long polished nails, have only ground to a halt once: to observe the three minutes' silence after Mao's death in 1976. This 'gambling cathedral' also comprises some 70 boutiques (jewellery shops, tailors, etc.), travel agencies, a counter for the China Bank, restaurants, saunas, cabarets, children's playrooms . . . Alluring prostitutes pace the corridors around the gambling rooms. You can do anything at the Lisboa without leaving its kilometres of corridors and galleries, its lifts that keep going up and its rooms where the well off and less well off of both sexes rub shoulders night and day: tourists in shorts, big-time gamblers who look like pimps, faceless crowds of those bitten by the gambling bug.

One of the Lisboa's best-known attractions is its Crazy Paris Show. This nude spectacle, inspired by the Crazy Horse Show

Macao's modern district.

in Paris, was one of Stanley Ho's ideas to attract customers. He began by introducing striptease acts on the ferries coming over from Hong Kong (the shows, like the gambling, began as soon as the boat left the British colony's territorial waters). Later, he wanted a high-calibre revue offering the kind of glamour you couldn't find elsewhere in Asia. Have failed to come to an arrangement with the Crazy Horse, he decided to set up his own revue. The inspiration behind the operation was a remarkable woman: Roberta Macarthy. This artistes' agent, the daughter of the deputy and mayor of Marseilles and the wife of a professor in the medical faculty, had been a singer in Paris in the 1950s under the name of Roberta. She approached the Crazy Horse's technicians and an acrobatic dancer, Guy Lesquoy, then on tour in the area with his own dance company. The Crazy Paris Show, a blend of musical revue and aesthetic nudity, was presented for the first time in 1979 in the small auditorium of the delightful Dom Pedro V Theatre. The show was supposed to run for two months, and has now been going for more than twenty years. It quickly transferred to a theatre in the Lisboa, where stiff police commissioners in Mao suits could be seen in among the crowd of peasants and Chinese workers mesmerized by the sight of naked blondes. According to Guy Lesquoy, who directed the dance troupe for twelve years, the Crazy Paris Show is now part of 'Macao's cultural heritage'.

How much money changes hands over the green baize of baccarat, roulette and '30 and 40' tables? How much is swallowed by the legions of slot machines known by the Chinese as 'tigers ravenous for coins'? The STDM has never disclosed its business figures. But before the handover, the company paid on average more than half a billion dollars each year in taxes to the Macao government, which represented 30 per cent of takings from gambling and 60 per cent of the city's revenue. The STDM's gambling franchise expired in 2001, and the arrival of Las Vegas companies in Macao has tolled the death knell for Stanley Ho's monopoly. The STDM will carry on managing its eleven casinos, but the new arrivals have projects of their own: large tourist complexes built as theme parks, one of which is supposed to recreate the atmosphere of Venice. Not even when it comes to gambling can Macao escape its fate as Europe's Disneyland on Chinese soil.

Until the mid-1990s, the STDM's monopoly on gambling in Macao ensured that a certain degree of order was maintained. But Stanley Ho has grown old, and, on the eve of the enclave being returned to Chinese administration, his empire has sparked rivalry in the underworld for control in the 'VIP rooms' ('privates') used by the biggest players. These VIP rooms are sub-let by the STDM to companies who manage their clientele: they take care of the gamblers' travelling and accommodation arrangements, offer protection and provide discounted chips as well as what the brochure calls 'attentive hostesses'. A lot of money of dubious origin crosses the green baize of the 'privates'.

This system of franchises (which is certainly lucrative for the STDM: some 'privates' pay ten million dollars a month in rent) has introduced foreign interest, notably that of the triads, to Macao's gambling scene. The name given by the British in the 19th century to a secret Chinese society (whose emblem was a triangle uniting Heaven, Earth and Man) has become the generic term used to designate Chinese organized crime. The activities of triads today are a world apart from social crime founded on a code of honour, and from the esoteric rituals of secret societies in imperial China, which practised religious and political dissidence in opposition to the Ching Dynasty during the upsurge leading to the 1911 revolution. Now they're just very dull crime syndicates. Traditionally, the triads called the shots in Macao as they did in Hong Kong. But the economic boom of the 1990s, triggered by the influx of Chinese capital (part of which ends up as laundered money) and by the casinos' stake, has increased their presence ten-fold; especially that of 14K, Hong Kong's most powerful criminal organization, now in open conflict with the more locally rooted Soi Fong, who count many Macanese in their ranks. Between 1997 and 1999, gang warfare resulted in about 30 deaths through accounts being settled in the street. The authorities are out of their depth: there are 4,000 triad members and 3,000 police officers. The arrest in a Lisboa suite in May 1998 of the head of 14K, Wan Kuok-tai, otherwise known as Broken Tooth Koi, while he was watching the film *Casino*, which is based on his life, did calm the game a little. Wan was accused of being behind an attack on Macao's chief of police, who had escaped by the skin of his teeth.

Maintaining order will be one of the hardest tasks for Macao's new authorities. The presence of the Chinese army in the enclave – which Beijing has demanded, contrary to stipulations in the 1987 handover accord, by invoking security problems – has forced the triads to lie low, if only temporarily.

View from castle.

Twilight of an Imaginary City

'Why is it so dark?' The hump-backed bridge linking the island of Taïpa is luminescent with street lights, like a shining path. Glistening new buildings are fixed in a still-sparkling skyline. In the cloaked silence of night comes 'from further off than the night' (Claude Roy) the rhythmic splashing of water from the fountain below, which proves reassuring. Just as these lights don't quite pierce the shadows, so the night, normally in league with the imagination, can't quite dissipate the melancholy of this final evening on the terrace of the Bela Vista.

I wonder if the city I've just been describing ever existed? Or was it just a place that faded in memory, an imaginary reconstruction of the past; like something two former lovers might surrender themselves to, without distinguishing between what really happened and what they simply dreamed up. What have I been looking for again in this city, when I knew the die was cast, that its protective spirit had already vanished and with it the spell it once wove, that feeling of happiness inspired by Macao 'the blessed'? Should I refrain from the bitter-sweet pleasure of acknowledging there is no longer a city here to be found?

A city is a fluid reality that blends the concrete with the imaginary. A concrete city overlays another one, invisible at first glance, that gradually sketches itself in as the physical configuration wears off. When this physicality blurs, the city becomes a prop to the imagination. In Macao the present used to mingle with a past that the city carried incrusted within it, 'like the lines in the palm of a hand', as Italo Calvino thought of it. The imaginary city resonated with reminders and remem-berings. It was a collection of forgotten lives, a long narrative

131

that unfolded like a roller painting as you walked along. Macao possessed the invaluable quality of making the visible city coincide with the imaginary one. And it was this that made you so fond of it as a place. Together with the fact, perhaps, that it brought you back to yourself.

Strolling through its streets, you couldn't help wondering about the ambitions and illusions that turned this fluffy bit of confetti on the steps of China into a landing stage for the possessed. If we're still walking in the footsteps of these ancients, what were they looking for or fleeing from? What have I come looking for, what am I fleeing from on the other side of the world? In this narrow stretch where so much of Europe and China used to co-exist, you could experience the physical sensation of travelling more than anywhere else.

This microcosm succinctly illustrated the encounter between two ways of being in the world. By juxtaposing them, Macao did away with geographical distances so that only cultural ones existed. This was a city where men and women born on opposite sides of the world rubbed shoulders and mixed, while the two civilizations to which they belonged remained strangers. Should we regret the failure of this encounter, deplore the resistance of this 'indomitable rock' the Jesuits could never fathom, having under-estimating its solidity and thought they'd found holes in illusory parallels between Western (Christian) thinking and Chinese thought, or should we offer our congratulations?

This kind of resistance is crucial to the 'taste for variety', made into an aesthetic by Victor Segalen. To 'taste variety' means shedding exoticism in the vein of Pierre Loti and his epigones, who appropriate 'otherness' in order to reintegrate it into their own understanding of the world and who 'remain shut off within their subjectivity like a drunkard in his alcoholic stupor' (Simon Leys). 'Everything has come to Europe and everything came from it. Or nearly everything.' There isn't space here to discuss Paul Valéry's aberrations. Let's just say that 'nearly' is critical, and that 'to experience your own humanity in the image of others' humanity', as Joseph

Needham put it, allows us to glimpse the extent to which our own culture is arbitrary, to perceive the historical aspect of our mental framework and to grasp that our 'reason' is perhaps less universal than we think.

Thought can be stimulated when tested against Difference, bringing with it other modes of intelligibility. 'Un-countries' (an expression coined by Chris Marker about Japan) involve us in a long and sometimes painful process of stripping down. The buildings we sagely construct within, ramparts with a unitary identity, lose their visible façade and begin to teeter. And it's in this slow disenchantment with yourself that you begin to understand why you have so far to travel; you understand that the fascination with going far away coincides with another voyage, deep inside you. Of course, you return from this other place, but the state of exile is now inside you. Macao was a stage along the way in this journey, and this is why its disappearance inspires such a feeling of loss.

Time is no longer suspended in a city where the hours used to hold no sway. A flash of eternity can't live on in unchanging monuments. These buildings linger like an incoherent collection of relics, for the collective movement that made sense of them has vanished like a watercourse whose path disappears into the sand. Macao has lost the ability to distil an historic experience in an imaginary one. A city accustomed to being overlooked has become prosaic, its past now a staged piece of theatre: a sad denial of what it once was.

'Why don't you stay, you images passing before the retina of my eyes?',wrote the exiled spirit of Camílio Pessanha in this city. The images have vanished. We should forget Macao 'the blessed' tenderly, like the memory of a vanished love we allow to fade, though moments of happiness may rise up unexpectedly from memories and dreams . . .

Photographic Acknowledgements

The author and publishers wish to express their thanks to the below sources of illustrative material and/or permission to reproduce it:

Lai Afong: p. 78; British Library Reproductions: pp. 65, 78, 90; Culver Pictures: pp. 6–7, 19, 24, 75 (top); HSBC Group Archives: pp. 8, 31; M.Leaman/Reaktion Books: pp. 17, 21, 32, 36, 47 (top), 75 (foot), 97, 119, 126, 130; the Macau Government Tourist Office: pp. 27, 47 (foot), 63, 100, 125.